Organization Theory
and Transnational
Social Movements

Organization Theory and Transnational Social Movements

Organizational Life and Internal Dynamics of Power Exercise within the Alternative Globalization Movement

Kléber Ghimire

LEXINGTON BOOKS

A division of
ROWMAN & LITTLEFIELD PUBLISHERS, INC.
Lanham • *Boulder* • *New York* • *Toronto* • *Plymouth, UK*

Published by Lexington Books
A division of Rowman & Littlefield Publishers, Inc.
A wholly owned subsidiary of The Rowman & Littlefield Publishing Group, Inc.
4501 Forbes Boulevard, Suite 200, Lanham, Maryland 20706
www.lexingtonbooks.com

Estover Road, Plymouth PL6 7PY, United Kingdom

British Library Cataloguing in Publication Information Available

Library of Congress Cataloging-in-Publication Data
Ghimire, K. B. (Kléber Bertrand)
  Organization theory and transnational social movements : organizational life
and internal dynamics of power exercise within the alternative globalization
movement / Kléber Ghimire.
       p. cm.
  Includes bibliographical references and index.
  ISBN 978-0-7391-6557-7 (hardcover : alk. paper) — ISBN 978-0-7391-6559-1
(ebook)
  1. Anti-globalization movement. 2. Globalization—Social aspects. 3. Social
movements. 4. Organizational behavior. 5. Organization. I. Title.
  HN17.5.G49 2011
  303.48'4—dc22   2010051971

Printed in the United States of America

Contents

Figures and Tables

FIGURES

TABLES

Abbreviations

ABONG	Brazilian Associations of Non-governmental Organizations (*Associação Brasileira de Organizações Não Governamentais*)
AER	Action for Economic Reforms
AFTA	Andean Free Trade Agreement
AGP	Peoples' Global Action (*Acción Global de los Pueblos*)
APEC	Asia Pacific Economic Cooperation
ARENA	Asian Regional Exchange for New Alternatives
ASEAN	Association of South-East Asia Nations
Attac	Association for the Taxation of Financial Transactions for the Aid of Citizens (*Association pour la taxation des transactions financières et pour l'aide aux citoyens*)
BBC	British Broadcasting Corporation
CADTM	Committee for the Abolition of Third World Debt (*Comité pour l'annulation de la dette du tiers monde*)
CBJP	Brazilian Commission of Justice and Peace (*Comissão Brasileira de Justiça e Paz*)
CCFD	Catholic Committe against Hunger and for Development (*Comité catholique contre la faim et pour le développement*)
CNCR	National Council of Rural Dialogue and Cooperation (*Conseil national de concertation et de coopération des ruraux*)
CONGAD	Council of NGOs for Development Support (*Conseil des ONG d'appui au développement*)
CSA	Continental Social Alliance
CUT	Unified Workers' Central (*Central Unica dos Trabalhadores*)
DEF	Davos Economic Forum

DPA	Presidential Anticorruption Delegation (*Delegación Presidencial Anticorrupción*)
EC	European Commission
EED	Church Development Service (*Evangelische Entwicklungs Dienst*)
FASE	Federation of Agencies for Social and Educational Assistance (*Federação de Órgãos Para Assistência Social e Educacional*)
FBOMS	Brazilian Forum of NGOs and Social Movements (*Fórum Brasileiro de ONGs e Movimentos Sociais*)
FC	Civil Forum (*Forum civil*)
FDC	Freedom for Debt Coalition
FSS	Senegalese Social Forum (*Forum social sénégalais*)
FTAA	Free Trade Area of the Americas
GATT	General Agreement on Tariffs and Trade
HIPC	Heavily Indebted Poor Countries
HIVOs	Humanist Institute for Cooperation with Developing Countries (*Humanistisch Instituut voor Ontwikkelingssamenwerking*)
IBASE	Brazilian Institute of Social and Economic Analyses (*Instituto Brasileiro de Análises Sociais e Econômicas*)
IC	International Council of the WSF
ICCO	Interchurch Organization for Development Cooperation (*Interkerkelijke Organisatie voor Ontwikkelingssamenwerking*)
IICG	International Initiative on Corruption and Governance
IMF	International Monetary Fund
INESC	Institute of Socioeconomic Studies (*Instituto de Estudios Socioeconómicos*)
INGOs	International NGOs
MAI	Multilateral Agreement on Investment
MDG	Millennium Development Goals
Misereor	German Catholic Bishop's Organization for Development Cooperation
MOPASSOL	Movement for Peace, Sovereignty and Solidarity among People (*Movimiento por la Paz, la Soberanía y la Solidaridad de los Pueblos*)
MST	Movement of Landless Rural Workers (*Movimento dos Trabalhadores Rurais sem Terra*)
NAFTA	North American Free Trade Agreement
NGOs	Non-governmental Organizations
OC	Brazilian Organizing Committee of the WSF
OECD	Organisation for Economic Co-operation and Development
OWINFS	Our World Is Not For Sale

PEACE	Platform of African Students for Fair Trade (*La Plateforme des étudiants africains pour le commerce équitable*)
Petrobras	Brazilian Oil Company (Petroleo Brasileiro)
RADI	African Network for Integrated Development (*Réseau africain pour le développement intégré*)
REPAOC	National Platforms of West and Central African NGOs (*Réseau des platesformes nationales d'ONG d'Afrique de l'Ouest et du Centre*)
RSJDH	Social network of Justice and Human Rights (*Rede Social de Justiça e Direitos Humanos*)
SAPs	Structural Adjustment Programs
SDC	Swiss Agency for Development and Cooperation
SIDA	Swedish International Development Cooperation Agency
SINPRO	Trade Union of Federal District Teachers (*Sindicato dos Professores do Distrito Federal*)
SNR	Stop the New Round Coalition
TAN	Transparency and Accountability Network
TI	Transparency International
TWN	Third World Network
UNACOIS	National Union of Senegalese Tradesmen and Industrialists (*Union nationale des commerçants et industriels du Sénégal*)
UNCTAD	United Nations Conference on Trade and Development
UNDP	United Nations Development Program
UNRISD	United Nations Research Institute for Social Development
UNSAS	National Union of Independent Trade Unions of Senegal (*Union nationale des sydicats autonomes du Sénégal*)
WSF	World Social Forum
WTO	World Trade Organization

Acknowledgments

From the time when I began to conceive a book project on the internal functioning and exercise of power within the alternative globalization movement from the perspective of the organization theory, I benefited sustained support from various sources. At the empirical level, I value a great deal the national information and other highly useful input offered to me by my previous research colleagues from Argentina, Bolivia, Senegal and the Philippines, namely Alejandro Grimson (Universidad Nacional de San Martín), Fernando Mayorga (Universidad Mayor de San Simón), Ibrahima Thioub (Université Cheikh-Anta Diop) and Teresa Tadem (University of the Philippines). With regard to the information on the transnational campaigns, too, I was fortunate to have close acquaintances with a certain number of leaders and militants within the World Social Forum, Attac France, debt movement and so forth.

At the logistical level, I had the rare opportunity to spend a quiet semester at the Centre d'études et de recherches internationales (CERIUM), University of Montreal, in 2008. The university library and intellectual atmosphere there was most congenial in beginning to elaborate the present text. I'm particularly grateful to Jean-Philippe Thérien and Dominique Caouette for their invitation to the university and keen interest in this work.

At the Université Stendhal Grenoble III, the contemporary social movements, including the alternative globalization movement, constituted a theme for a faculty colloquium in 2009, organized under the framework of a monthly seminar series on Humanism and Conflictuality. In this seminar as well as during the latter months, my colleagues Marc Troisvallets, Rolande Borrelly, Patrice Allard and Alda Del Forno (Université Pierre Mendès

France) offered thoughtful comments on the broad analytical scope of the present book.

In regard to the present text, Teresa Tadem amiably checked the chapters that concern the four country studies. Shigeko Fukai (University of Chiba) generously read the entire text and provided me with several important comments. Michele Bernini (School of African and Oriental Studies) also read certain parts of the text.

To all of them I would like to express my sincere gratitude.

This said, the line of arguments developed and any of the shortcomings appearing in the book naturally remain my own entire responsibility.

I

GENERAL INTRODUCTION

1

Organization Theory, Social Movements and Power

"Quoi qu'on disent certains hypocrites, le pouvoir est le premier des plaisirs."[1]

—Stendhal[2]

Kuhn and Beam state that "every social system is an organization" (Kuhn and Beam 1982: xiii). In this sense, any social, political, economic or cultural institution or action, whether structured or informal, is an "organization." Social movements can easily be described as organizations. Indeed, according to Touraine, social movements are "the heart of the social life" and they occur "in a permanent manner" (Touraine 1978: 47). Social movements are both processes and actors that commonly aim at advancing certain causes, interests or pursuits. Their societal impacts, either positive or negative, can at times be considerable. For these reasons, it is quite legitimate to ask how social movements emerge in a given context, as well as how they internally function in their quest to accomplish their broader and specific objectives. Furthermore, as can be imagined, social movements frequently mutate or entirely new ones may emerge, thus the need to a constant renewal on the existing theoretical and analytical parameters. This work takes into consideration that the "alternative globalization movement" (known initially as the anti-globalization movement) is a social organization of a "new genre" and that the empirical and theoretical bases for understanding its composition, key objectives, modes of operation and inner power relations remain thus far largely deficient.

Beginning from the work of Weber on the bureaucracy at the beginning of the 20th century and supplemented considerably by North-American

3

sociologists and political scientists before and after World War II, the phenomenon of "organization" has been an object of ample studies and analyses. Drawing on information and insights from numerous disciplines, notably sociology, economy and political science, a relatively rich corpus of knowledge exists on the structure, rules, functioning, division of tasks and efficiency of different types of actors and organizations. Yet much of this observation relates mainly to the Western industrial societies; it is concerned primarily with the question of organizational efficiency or outcome; formal or structured sets of organizations such as public administration or business enterprises remain its essential methodological focus; and it is limited, to a great extent, mainly to the economics field. Accordingly, social movements, albeit not totally neglected, do not constitute the core body of this literature.

Within this intellectual tradition, even when social movements are considered, much of the attention is paid to the issues concerning their economic rationality, interest or effectiveness. This is not at all surprising given the fact that the development of organization theory was closely associated with the periods of brisk economic activities. For example, during the end of the 19th and beginning of the 20th centuries when the early thinkers and economic entrepreneurs (e.g., Weber, Taylor, Fayol and Ford) began to ponder about the organizational principles from the point of economic efficiency, Europe and North America were experiencing a major phase of industrial and economic impulsion based on the development of innovative technologies—notably petrochemicals and electricity, organization of production in large factories, greater use of stock markets, growing worldwide demands for manufactured goods, and so on. Likewise, a large quantity of specialized management literature emerged in the 1980s and 1990s—a period marked by an accelerated liberalization in financial and economic sectors, an ascendency of transnational enterprises, increased internationalization of production and sales of commercial goods and the rapid development in new information technologies. Much of the literature, written in great quantities by business consultants, economists and economic sociologists, has been concerned primarily with the question of how to achieve an enhanced organizational management involving human, technological and financial resources that would produce in due course an optimum economic return for the enterprise.

To these general observations, we may also add that the development of the organization theory in many ways directly reflected a historical trend in the shift of economic power from Europe to North America that ensued from the end of the 19th century. This endowed the latter region (or more precisely the United States) to assertively push for an ideology of free market economy, impose the United States dollar as world currency, preside over leading financial institutions such as the International Monetary Fund (IMF) and World Bank and promote worldwide American economic investment through a network of powerful multinational companies. Sociology steadily found a fertile ground in the United States, although the discipline seemingly chose to ignore these wider international dimensions of power alterations and the subsequent United States' domination. In 1950s and 1960s, numerous important attempts were made in the United States to investigate the composition, strategies and political influence of "pressure groups" such as civil rights organizations, labor unions, women's movements, churches, professional and private associations. Nevertheless, many of these studies opted to highlight the rational nature of economic and political strategies of social actors, independently from their ideological influence or wider ethical concerns.

Generally speaking, the arena of economic behaviors tended to receive the foremost attention. Mancur Olson argued that social mobilizations were all about logical self-interested economic behaviors. He insisted that "no one is surprised when individual businessmen seek higher profits, when individual workers seek higher wages, or when individual consumers seek lower prices" (Olson 1965: 1). Anchoring largely on this conception, a whole new generation of scholars emerged in the 1970s around the much-known theory of "resource mobilization," suggesting that the organizational structure and strength of a social movement depended essentially upon its strategy to mobilize essential resources (see, for example, McCarthy and Zald 1973). These scholars recognized that resources could be multiple. Nevertheless, the dimension of economic resources tended to receive appreciably more attention.

The question that arises is: Are social movements simply or predominantly extensions of the individual *homos economicus* behavior? In the European context in the 1970s and in the early 1980s, authors such as Touraine and Melucci emphasized the emergence of "new social movements" on such issues as peace, ecology, women's rights, and so forth, and led essentially by the middle class, professional and academic people. They also argued that, although these movements sought to strengthen their group identity and interests, there was a significant concern for broader societal values such as the protection of the environment and gender equality (Touraine 1985: 749–787; Melucci 1985: 663–716). Bourdieu argued that social movements in the European context have had the role of even "civilizing" the market economy "while largely contributing to its efficacy" (Bourdieu 2001: 16). In other words, to these authors, social movements were not merely the result of a rational and calculated economic logic among social actors. More crucially, these actors commonly attached importance to world peace, justice and many other similar fundamental principles.

This book intends to present a critical panorama on the organizational life and internal working of the alternative globalization movement. We will see in the subsequent pages that, although the various participating organizations and groups may have differing origins, motivations and strategies, as a combined force, the movement is deeply concerned about the negative effects of the recent global financial, economic and technological integration on people's general well-being, social cohesion and peace. It is also greatly concerned about the diminished role of the State in managing the economy. Accordingly, the movement deems as necessary to bring about significant changes in the present economic models and global power structures. By and large, Bourdieu saw the movement possessing five important characteristics:

1. refusal to get organized in traditional forms of political mobilizations led by political parties
2. invention of symbolic as well as concrete actions
3. rejection to the neoliberal politics promoted by large institutional investors and multinational companies
4. amalgamation between particularity (working on a specific topic or in a country) and internationalist view
5. exaltation of solidarity with popular struggles (Bourdieu 2001: 59–61).

These different yet mutually connected features illustrate that the alternative globalization movement is largely a value-oriented organization. It displays a certain sense of political responsibility. It seeks to work towards building a new democratic architecture and calls for increased solidarity. In any event, there are no obvious or primary economic motives behind the mounting and animating of a movement of this nature. Unlike most social movements in the past, the alternative globalization movement also has the intent of functioning at national as well as global levels covering both industrial and developing societies. It aims at functioning as an aggregated force, yet largely in an informal manner. In particular, it calls for mobilization across social groups representing such forces as youth, women, urban labor and the peasantry. Some of these dimensions are set forth in more detail in the following section. We may however note at this stage that many of the aspects that are intrinsic to the current alternative globalization movement do not fall into any typical areas of investigation within the organization theory analysis.

Informed organization theorists have begun to recognize this lacuna in recent years. For example, the journal of *Administrative Science Quarterly* brought together in its September 2002 issue a number of scholars to reflect upon the evolving themes within the field of organization studies. Hinings and Greenwood, two leading authors in this volume, allow that the "issues of organizational design" and "the effect of organizational action on the shaping of societies" should constitute an important domain of thought and studies "in newer topics of organizations and the environment, gender and diversity and globalization" (Hinings and Greenwood 2002: 416). Pertinently they ask, "Do the new organizational forms that have arisen over the past two decades and that continue to emerge have any similar implications for the distribution of power and privilege internally and externally?" On the whole, they recommend that "the concept of interest should be a central one in such studies" (ibid. 418).

This work is formulated in some ways directly in response to this call; and parallel to this, the author was also fortunate to have the opportunity to engage in an international research project in this area during the early 2000s (details below). Having said this, the purpose of the study has been to throw light in particular on the question of the "organizational design," and only occasional references would be made to the dimension of the "effect of organizational action." We believe the organizational design in itself is a substantial field of enquiry, considering specially that information and analyses over the alternative globalization movement on this specific aspect have so far tended to be utterly partial. It therefore appears necessary to learn, describe and assess the composition of different groups represented within the movement, the nature of their alliance and coordination of different activities, organizational coherence, internal communication, resources availability, representation systems, short and long-term objectives, strategies and political visions, as well as relations with authorities (or adversaries). Predictably, this implied the need to design an empirically grounded work.

We should further note that any serious discussion on the internal structure of a social movement must invariably include the question of how organizational regulations are formulated and put into practice. In other words, how is hierarchy conceived? What are the prime methods of delegation of important responsibilities? Within the chain of command, how do leading individuals or groups justify their positions and the established modes of action? Evidently, many of them would have differing priorities or motives. They may also have differing ability to wield influence and authority. As a matter of fact, the leading individuals or actors may not only be able to attain important organizational power, but also possess the capacity to plainly justify their legitimacy through diverse means even when their actions are contradictory or designed primarily to suit their narrow interests. Plato, referring to the propensity of the prominent political leaders to frequently justify their unjust acts through courage, vigor, friends and personal wealth, described this as "to appear to be just while not being so" (Plato 1966: 110).

To Hinings and Greenwood, as noted above, it is particularly fundamental that "the concept of interest" is fully taken into consideration in organizational analysis. What these authors denote as "interest" in actual fact is "power"—a notion that has undoubtedly remained an important domain of debate within organization theory as a whole.[3] Briefly stating, three main typologies of power have been described in the literature, often representing differing philosophical or political roots and interpretations. The first typology defines power in relation to the superiors and subordinates. To Xenophon, for example, this is something like "the natural obedience of herds to their shepherds."[4] In other words, just as the herder guides and protects the animals knowing where the good pasture is, in social life, elites are supposed to distinguish themselves from the mass by their exceptional qualities, and as such, they have the mandate to lead the mass. The result of this situation, as it can be expected, is the gradual emergence and crystallization of tensions between those who rule and those who are subjected to obey.

The second form of power is the "production of intended effects" (Russell 1985: 25). Here, unlike the first form of power, persuasions and manipulations are important tools commonly employed by leaders. There is notably an absence of a direct coercion. Besides, given the risk of resistance by subordinates or their abilities to exercise certain influence within the production system in a variety of ways,[5] a plain coercion can become largely counterproductive from the point of view of the organizational efficiency.

In the third form, and somewhat related to the second, power is perceived more as "social relations" within the organization, as opposed to the notion of power as "substance" (cf. applicable in the case of the first two categories outlined above). In other words, the authority is acquired through "micro-mechanisms of power," such as the discourses of truth and possession of knowledge (Foucault 1994: 404).

Obviously, it makes little sense talking of the first typology of power associated with the notion of command-obedience relationships with regard to the alternative globalization movement. The movement is informal, and perceptibly, there is no central despotic authority to dominate and subjugate the individuals and groups which make up the movement. However, the last two interpretations of power have vital relevance to the examination of the alternative globalization movement. In order to demonstrate that the movement is alive and going, a number of basic activities must be carried out. In consequence, this gives rise to the use of power by selected individuals or groups. Furthermore, the exercise of authority may be accompanied by numerous micro-mechanisms of power, such as the use of intellectual capital, expedient contacts with the media or ability to raise financial resources.

What seems particularly pertinent to recognize in this regard is the alternative globalization movement's proper interpretation of power. Notably the movement considers the concentration of power inside the organization to be totally unacceptable. It draws lessons from the history of social movements to suggest that political parties and labor unions tended to give rise to the seizure of power by a few, creation of a heavy bureaucracy and lack of transparency in their operation. Logically then a new organizational structure must emerge avoiding rigid forms of hierarchy and encouraging a more diffused process of power sharing. So what is in actual fact the contour and content of this imaginative and informal organizational structure? How is its overall functioning and what are the related outcomes? In specific, how do different interests and power relations manifest, as well as become gradually incorporated within much of the organizational structure and operation activities?

GENERAL FEATURES OF THE ALTERNATIVE GLOBALIZATION MOVEMENT

There is now a sizeable literature on the alternative globalization movement, and in recent years this seems to be growing considerably. Much of this is, however, written by research students and academics who have been engaged with the movement in one manner or another. Expectedly, this group of authors has tended to give a generally promising image of the movement. This is, for example, the case with many of the university intellectuals associated with the Association for the Taxation of Financial Transactions for the Aid of Citizens (Attac[6]). For example, *Le petit alter: Dictionnaire altermondialiste*, edited by Attac, mentions that the alternative globalization movement has the crucial aim of working towards "the emancipation of humanity." And the movement would do this, as the explanation goes, by enhancing human dignity, deepening democracy, protecting the ecosystems, conceiving new forms of solidarity and sharing, as well as respecting the diversity of cultures, ways of living and traditions. This publication nevertheless also recognizes that the question which greatly conditions the capacity of the movement "to incarnate a true project of human emancipation for the 21st century is to know if alternative globalization will succeed to consenting to the preoccupations traditionally called social, historically resulting from labor movement and ecological concerns" (Attac 2006: 28–29).

Numerous prominent scholars have also generally allowed a favorable opinion on the movement. We saw above Bourdieu generally eulogizing

the alternative globalization movement. In the same vein, Touraine infers that "the alternative globalization movement occupies a place as
important as socialism during the first decades of the industrial society"
(Touraine 2005: 47–48). Even more remarkably, the American erudi-
tion that normally limited itself to studying civic movements and social
structures in North America in the past has taken a growing interest in the
movement (McAdam, McCarthy and Zald 1996; Keck and Sikkink 1998;
Guidry, Kennedy and Zald 2000; Tarrow 2005; Smith 2007). Analyzing
the movement from their usual standpoint of the Resource Mobilization
Theory, they attempt to demonstrate how "globalization brings important
resources to the mobilizational efforts of movements" (Guidry, Kennedy
and Zald 2000: 2). Taken as a whole, is alternative globalization a new
cosmopolitanism, representing largely an atypical historical trajectory and
political philosophy?

A few authors have begun to draw attention to the various ambiguities
embedded in the alternative globalization movement. Wieviorka asks,
"Beyond reactions and sentiments, has not the time come to found our ap-
preciation on the reasoning, that-is-to-say on the knowledge and analysis?"
(Wieviorka 2003: 7). He goes on to assert that the movement embraced
the peril in three dimensions: first, it gets taken over by the left sponsoring
hypercritical view, rejecting all negotiations with the system; second, with
the care to put forward workable propositions, the movement goes into the
logic of offering expertise, thereby making it lose its contestation dynamics;
and third, the movement gets influenced by diverse forms of identity re-
treat, including communitarian, fundamentalist, sectarian and totalitarian
radicalization (ibid. 45–49).

Within this intellectual strand, we may also mention the writings of
Martin, Metzger and Pierre, which argue that the alternative globalization
movement has no real capacity "to control the historicity of the transnational society in economic and cultural control given its small number
and multiple and often contradictory projects on the field and level of
intervention sought" (Martin, Metzger and Pierre 2006: 597–508). These
authors do not believe that the movement has compelled the leading
international institutions such as the World Trade Organization (WTO),
International Monitory Fund (IMF) or the European Commission (EC) to
make "significantly different choices" in their policy orientations; instead
these institutions have simply brought "modifications of their institutional
communication, which in the end just seems to reinforce their legitimacy"
(ibid. 510).

In more recent years, this evolution has especially been perceptible with
respect to the media announcement and agenda items considered by the
Davos Economic Forum (DEF)—the annual event that brings together
many powerful world political and economic leaders. The issues of poverty,

income disparities, transparency of financial markets and social responsibility of multinational companies commonly raised by the alternative globalization movement are no longer a taboo for the DEF. As a matter of fact,
in its 2008 report, the DEF went on to declare that the "growth of economic
opportunity as a result of globalization must be combined with a sense of
values centered on the notions of justice and freedom."[7] This language is
astonishingly similar to that often employed within the alternative globalization movement.

Certainly, making declarations is not a difficult exercise. What ultimately
counts is how such declarations are put into effect. Clearly, in its overall
mandate, group representation and administrative configuration, the DEF
is hardly comparable to the alternative globalization movement. Figure 1
summarizes the principal traits of the alternative globalization movement.
With respect to its core political philosophy, the movement is deeply concerned with the consequences of the current form of a rapid and inequi-
table economic globalization. In particular, it questions the ability of liberal market economy to guarantee prosperity and social protection for the
majority of the world population. On the contrary, it believes unsupervised
economic liberalization can cause considerable damage to the well-being of
the common people and their physical environment.

FIGURE 1.   THE GENERAL CHARACTERISTICS OF THE ALTERNATIVE GLOBALIZATION MOVEMENT

Political philosophy	Pragmatic antagonism against the present neoliberal economic and political systems
Organizational structure	Based on non-hierarchical, informal and occasional cooperation and alliances among networks of ideologically and geographically diverse NGOs and social movements
Means	Popular and worldwide mobilizations, especially at international events
Methods of operation	Nonviolent and persuasive

In spite of this opinion, the movement does not want to "throw out
the baby with the bathwater." It infers that globalization can be positive
if built on the principles of justice as well as mutual respect and solidarity
among peoples. This explains why in the early 2000s the movement was
swiftly renamed from "anti" to "alternative." Conceiving of a pragmatic
radicalism was also meant to leave a certain degree of room for contacts and

possible dialogues with potential allies (for example, broad-minded State elites, United Nations organizations, etc.). According to Gustave Massiah, a notable figure within the alternative globalization movement in France, such alliances could take place with a broad range of social forces standing against hegemony and war, fundamentalist tendencies and capitalist and productionist notions and practices. They could notably include the ecologists and socio-liberals opposing neo-liberalism (Massiah 2005:149), in addition to the forces from the left which nevertheless remain the principal architect of the movement.

In terms of its organizational structure, the alternative globalization movement is a loose network of associative organizations such as development NGOs, social movements, international campaigns, social forums, and so forth. The movement has no central administration, designated central leaders, or adherents. It basically functions as an informal and open space of gathering and affinity for willing individuals, groups and organizations. Accordingly, there is no specific organizational obligation attached to those who may want to join the movement. In another word, anyone can enter, leave or re-enter the movement at any moment.

The movement's followers are often highly fragmented along ideological lines—originating from the extreme left to the ecologists and Christian democrats. The minimum denominator to become part of the movement is their common opposition to the present neoliberal market economy and its negative consequences, as well as their desire to install the primacy of politics and social actors over economy.

Geographically, too, the movement seeks to stretch from the North to the South, as well as from transnational to the national level, albeit with mixed success, as we shall see subsequently.

Wieviorka believes that the alternative globalization movement has two distinct sides: an offensive side that aims at promoting a counter-project against the present economic system and a defensive side that attempts to tackle the degradation in the living and working conditions of the common people (Wieviorka 2003: 28–29). Perceptibly, the movement proposes to deploy somewhat differing means to achieve these two different goals. The organization of global forums and public demonstrations at the international conferences are some of the movement's prime means to promote its counter-project. This is combined with advocacy, lobbying activities and the strategy to influence the media and public opinion. However, since a strong emphasis is put on the identity building and opponents are harshly criticized, it becomes difficult to enter into any serious discussions or negotiations with the opponents or public authorities. Even in the case of the defensive actions, according to Wieviorka, the movement "frequently oscillates between the apathy and total rupture, with no great capacity to install itself on a negotiating space" (ibid. 29). On the whole, the movement seeks to "communicate" its main ideas, as well as put forward its demands to the adversary, frequently interposed by the media a few times with influential personalities, but it seldom enters into direct negotiations.

Finally, the alternative globalization movement lays emphasis wholly on persuasive and non-violent methods. In any event, there is no call as such for organized mass revolt or taking up of arms. This is the case even with the small groups of extreme-left and libertarian (anarchist) movements that can be found intermittently joining the movement.[8] Evidently, the majority of the forces or groups rallying behind the alternative globalization movement is comprised of pragmatic radicals who want to avoid violence. Consenting to peaceful means helps them, among others, to present an acceptable image of the movement before the wider public, State authorities and international media. Indeed, the sporadic violence that was witnessed at international gatherings in the earlier days of the movement's trajectory was soon deplored by its key leaders (see, for example, George 2002: 111; Cassen 2004).

Social movements' criticism of the dominant economical, socio-cultural and political system is not any exceptional phenomenon. Nor is its geographical extension so uncommon. The trade unions and communist party–related movements mobilized a great number of people around the world from the end of the 19th century. The Red Cross was founded in 1863 as a worldwide network with the mandate to assist and protect victims and refugees of armed conflicts. Likewise, the antislavery movement and the campaign for women's suffrage are seen by some academics as being "historical frontrunners" to recent transnational movements (Keck and Sikkink 1998: 2). Prior to these transnational movements, the Christian and Muslim religions had emerged with a strong social message and they gained an intercontinental character several centuries ago (Braudel 1987: 187–150, 421–496). According to Mintzberg, a typical religious organization is animated by missionary fervor based on the sharing of a common ideological principle among its followers. Moreover, its organizational arrangement is unstructured and largely decentralized (Mintzberg 2003: 484–491).

Many these characteristics are manifest within the alternative globalization movement. But the organization is also significantly different in a number of areas. First, the ideological suppleness that it pursues is rather uncommon among the past social movements linked to religious, labor or party politics. Second, away from the previous practices of betting on a single set of organization, the entire conception of the alternative globalization movement is built on the principle of networking with the prospect of mobilizing resources across multiple social organizations and movements. The third salient aspect characterizing the movement is its fervent advocacy for maintaining an informal and diffused form of organizational hierarchy. The basic rationale of this is to ensure an extensive and egalitarian political participation and decision-making process among diverse organizations and social groups constituting the movement.

Overall, the movement displays a great deal of idealism for constructing a new humanism and world order. No doubt similar optimism was fervently expressed by political parties and trade union movements of the left (after the triumph and subsequent questioning on the ability of liberal economic and political thoughts and practice to offer a caring and equitable society) in the late 19th and early 20th centuries. It is in this sense, precisely, Touraine compared the alternative globalization movement to socialism during the early years of the European industrialization process characterized by deplorable employment and living conditions of the working people and mounting social conflicts. In comparison to socialism, the alternative globalization has yet to prove its longevity—particularly in terms of the wider societal relevance of its philosophical belief, as well as magnitude and durability of its social actions in concrete contexts. More significantly, despite initial displays of democratic spirit and sanguine ideals, in practice, the essential outcome may be disparate or even contradictory. In other words, while grand principles may continually be emphasized, many officious and power-grabbing propensities could emerge. It should be recalled that Plato over two millennium ago already perceived the danger of democracy allowing the leadership to "nurture and expand power" for its own benefits (Plato 1966: 325).

As such, it is pertinent to know how these diverse positions and facets of the alternative globalization movement actually fair in reality. How are the internal structure, decision-making process and "managerial" culture created? What are the outcomes of these various aspects on the general exercise of organizational power? How do different individuals and social organizations making the movement bring to bear their influence? More precisely, is this influence utilized in a democratic fashion? Or is it that the movement represents in essence an "idealistic" project accompanied by an attempt to develop various "novel" forms of organizational configurations and working, but at the end of the day it cannot deflect such happenings anyway? In order to understand why and how these manifold questions arise, lets us consider in some details the general organizational composition of the movement.

DIFFERENT CONSTITUENTS OF THE ALTERNATIVE GLOBALIZATION MOVEMENT AND THE FOCUS OF THIS BOOK

Owing to the fact that the alternative globalization movement is a broad "network of networks" and it emphasizes an extensive representation of politically and geographically diverse groups, enumerating the composition of the movement is not an easy affair. Wieviorka outlines the structure of the alternative globalization movement to be composed of three principal sources: action-oriented international NGOs (INGOs); civil society mobilizations that take place around international events or conferences; and single-cause oriented international campaigns (Wieviorka 2003: 22–23). Regarding the first group, one instantaneously thinks of well-established transnational organizations with specific mandates and areas of intervention such as Amnesty International (human rights), Green Peace (environment), Oxfam (humanitarian assistance), etc. These organizations are no longer new forces in international advocacy activities, but they have become one of the crucial supporters of the alternative globalization movement. For example, Oxfam is the core financial supporter to the World Social Forum (WSF) since its inception (Diaz 2006: 96). On the whole, most of these international non-governmental organizations hold more of a practial or realistic vision of the world, rather than seeking to alter political and economic structures completely.

The civil society mobilizations around important international events such as those in Seattle, Genoa, Cancun, Porto Alegre and alike frequently involve the organization of protest marches, demonstration of force and expression of antagonism towards the liberal economic and commercial policies of the leading world institutions like the WTO, IMF, World Bank, G8, or the military and political hegemony of certain countries, notably the United States. Humanitarian NGOs, social movements, trade unions, religious and cultural associations, professional organizations and academic bodies are the usual principal actors behind these mobilizations. The core activities of these initiatives remain short-term, at times lasting only a couple of days. Nevertheless, these events have also frequently permitted the participating individuals, groups and associations to establish salutary regional and international linkages, with a few of these relations apparently lasting for a considerable period of time (Ghimire 2010: 1–21).

The last group that makes up the alternative globalization movement is international campaigns. Seeking to advance a particular cause or proposition at the global level such as the elimination of land mines, reduction of developing countries' debt, protection of the rainforests, etc., these campaigns draw wide-ranging social forces, including well-known personalities from the media or political circle. To promote their principal pleas more effectively, these campaigns look to lobbying considerate government elites and representatives from international organizations such as the United Nations. Some of these campaigns may come to an end following the achievement (or non-achievement) of their principal demands, but many of them have tended to go on—at times harboring internal divisions, declines and new mutations.

In this book, we take up two essential categories constituting the alternative globalization movement: transnational campaigns and the World Social Forum (see Figure 2 on their principal characteristics). Many international action-oriented NGOs (i.e., the first type of actors outlined above) are also present within these two categories, on occasion remaining their vital backbone, as we shall observe in the later discussions. We begin by giving a few illustrative details on each of the selected two categories. This information, albeit clearly descriptive, is nonetheless essential to understand the complexity in which certain forms of organizational structures or mechanisms of power relations emerge within the alternative globalization movement.

FIGURE 2. THE PRINCIPAL TRAITS OF THE SELECTED TRANSNATIONAL CAMPAIGNS AND WORLD SOCIAL FORUM

	Main Organizations Behind	Principal Social Base	Key Claims / Demands	Level of Contacts with the Public Authority
Transnational Campaigns				
debt relief campaign	Jubilee 2000 and its variants	church bodies	reduction/ cancellation of debt for developing countries	considerable contacts with Christian and social democratic political parties in Europe
trade justice campaign	Oxfam and its sister organizations	NGOs	removal of unfair trade rules and barriers	occasional links with government ministers and political parties
currency transaction tax campaign	Attac	anti-neoliberal development economists/ academic institutions	universal tax on foreign exchange and regulation of markets	direct/ indirect contacts with certains political parties,

	Main Organizations Behind	Principal Social Base	Key Claims / Demands	Level of Contacts with the Public Authority
				parliaments and development agencies to elaborate global taxation ideas, plans or legislation
anti-corruption campaign	Transparency International	human rights activists, jurists, journalists	corruption control	substantial collaborative links with international agencies, business communities, and government authorities in view of successfully implementing international conventions against corruption
World Social Forum				
	Brazilian/European NGOs and social movements	NGOs/social movements	Indistinct demands for significant changes in the current forms of world political and economic governance	Salutary contacts with the Brazilian government and left-wing political parties in Europe and Latin America

INTERNATIONAL CAMPAIGNS

Debt Relief Campaign

Debt relief is a highly perceptible transnational campaign; and according to some observers, it has become "a privileged object of engagement" within the whole of the alternative globalization movement (Agrikoliansky, Fillieule and Mayer 2005: 68). A variety of networks of NGOs, trade unions, academic centers and similar social organizations have commonly rallied behind the debt campaign with the common belief that the debt problem was seriously affecting both national economies and the living conditions of ordinary citizens in developing countries. The issue of debt has remained particularly high on the agenda of the Christian charity organizations, with the mobilization structure stretching from local churches to the Vatican. In addition to engaging in mass mobilization, campaigners organize "debt tribunals"[9] aimed at recording the negative effects of debt on the suffering of the common people and national consultations on debt—including the elaboration of alternative legislative measures that could potentially help the country in question to better cope with the debt burden.

In order to create public or media effect, debt campaigners commonly solicit endorsements from celebrities such as Bono, Billy Graham, Harry Belafonte, or the archbishop Desmond Tutu. Indeed, this method of operation has confirmed to be quite successful in influencing the debates on debt policies of the leading international financial institutions, as well as cancellation of some of the bilateral debts by Northern countries. The Jubilee 2000 was distinctly the height of the accomplishment (Collins, Gariyo and Burdon 2001: 135–148) with considerable impact on the public mind and media, and, to a lesser extent, on the government institutions in certain countries—notably the United Kingdom. However, the success of the Jubilee 2000 as a unified worldwide movement proved transient, with a major dissection taking place around the question of whether debt cancellation should be partial or total.

The consequence of this divergent position was that an important group of activists went ahead creating the Jubilee South (with the headquarters in Manila). This organization argued for a need to exert maximum pressure on national leaders in developing countries so that they may act collectively to repudiate the debt. Manifestly, this group took a more militant line than the economic and moralist approach of the initial Jubilee 2000, which also combined the issues of charity and debt forgiveness with public awareness raising and indirect pressure on the authorities and financial institutions. Within the Jubilee South, some fringe groups have gone as far as insisting that the debt relief measures should also include reparations of the damage caused by debt burden on the national environment, society and economy in the developing world (see Keet 2001: 243–267; Tagle and Sehm-Patomäki 2007: 25).

Trade Justice Movement

The trade justice movement calls for a fundamental change in the unjust rules and institutions governing international trade. In specific, it has sought to draw attention to the basic problem relating to the continued erection of trade barriers for Southern products in Northern countries, as well as undermining of Southern industrial and agricultural capacity through export dumping by rich countries. The Trade Justice Movement (United Kingdom), with affiliations to over 50 civic organizations, is clearly one of the leading international networks. Oxfam (International/Great Britain) has been closely associated with this initiative from its inception. But the Oxfam has also established its own constituencies in many countries (both in the North and the South), particularly in seeking to launch its worldwide "market access campaign." The organization has persistently argued that the removal of trade barriers in rich countries would produce substantial benefits for small producers in poor countries (Oxfam 2002: 3–16).

However, a certain number of ecological and Third World militant groups have criticized the Oxfam campaign in particular and the trade justice movement in general by saying that more emphasis should be given to the development of local and national self-reliance economies rather than to an export-led trade (*The Ecologist*, July–August 2002). The Focus on the Global South (based in Manila), another network on trade issues, stated that the trade position of Oxfam did not challenge the WTO-led neoliberal globalization process associated with many negative effects on Southern producers.[10] In addition to this, various social and political networks have become increasingly active in North and South America in opposing trade liberalization policies that have been promoted in recent years, particularly within the framework of the North American Free Trade Agreement (NAFTA) and the Free Trade Area for the Americas (FTAA).

Some of these networks have also sought to create alliances with political elites from powerful emerging countries such as Brazil, India and South Africa. This development was particularly perceptible during the 2003 WTO Cancun trade negotiation, but also surfaced at the trade negotiation meetings in Hong Kong 2005, Geneva 2006 and Potsdam 2007. Many these regional and transnational networks and a certain number of governments have continued to express their disapproval over the need to have to open up the strategic agricultural and industrial sectors in developing countries under WTO accords, as well as persistent provision of farm and export subsidies in rich nations (*Third World Resurgence* 2003).

Currency Transaction Tax

Among transnational campaigns, the currency transaction tax or Tobin tax movement has gained repute, in part due to the rapid growth in financial speculation and volatility of markets affecting the world economy. It is argued that a small universal tax on foreign exchange earnings would make financial market more transparent, as well as create an important source of public financing for social development in poorer countries. Patomäki believes the currency transaction campaign draws together both the reformist (those appealing for "more development aid" contributions from developed countries) and radical networks (those associated with the idea of "another world is possible" thus arguing for significant transformation in international economic and political systems) (Patomäki 2007: 11–12).

Despite the doubts expressed by some economists and financial specialists regarding the viability of the currency transaction tax proposal on both technical and political grounds (Wolf 2002; Giordano 2004: 23–24), a number of governments, parliamentarians and political parties have expressed support for the general idea of a global taxation (Paul and Wahlberg 2002: 12–13). Some scholars have also referred to the case of the airline-ticket solidarity tax (set up in recent years with the initiative of France and Brazil for the treatment of HIV, malaria and tuberculosis) to indicate that workable methods could be found (Uemura 2007: 15–17).

Numerous development NGOs, church organizations and trade unions have rallied behind the idea of an international taxation. The Attac movement, founded in France in June 1998, is a leading network in this field. It calls for the introduction of Tobin tax to regulate the financial market and also to counter the "dictatorship of the market." It has established affiliations in most European countries and maintained links in many other countries in Latin America, Africa and Asia, with a total membership reaching over 100,000.[11] Even though a number of similar networks with focus on Tobin tax have emerged in other countries—namely in Canada, the United States, the United Kingdom and Germany—Attac, with the use of academic intellect, media and increased co-ordination of activities with different movements and organizations is by far the most influential movement in this particular area. Significantly, in many countries, it has gained the stature of being the prime focal points of the alternative globalization movement.

Anti-Corruption Campaign

Corruption takes place in numerous forms such as bribery, embezzlement, fraud, extortion, trafficking of influence, money laundering and obstruction of justice (Nieto 2004: 64–65; Nye 1967: 417). Some scholars believe corruption is "a particular concern for developing countries because it undermines economic growth, discourages foreign investment and reduces the resources available for infrastructure, public services and anti-poverty programmes" (Robinson 1998: 2). Others have ascertained a direct correlation between corruption and legitimacy of democracies (Seligson 2006: 402). Overall, the anticorruption phenomenon has been a recurrent theme among bilateral and international agencies, leading to the development of such schemes as the UN Convention against Corruption 2003, Inter-American Convention against Corruption 1996 and the Organisation for Economic Co-operation and Development (OECD) Convention on Combating Bribery of Foreign Public Officials in International Business Transactions in 2005—with human rights NGOs, jurists, journalists and academic networks taking active part in the debate as well as working towards the implementation of many these international conventions.

Transparency International (TI) is the leading transnational anti-corruption campaign organization. It has brought together many civic organizations as well as sought to actively collaborate with government agencies, donor organizations and business associations (Galtung 2000: 17–44). Most notably, since 1995, it has published annual corruption perception indices seeking to bring the issues of corruption to the forefront of the public debate in a regular manner. TI has maintained national chapters in over 80 countries that work towards reducing corruption, including the monitoring of performance of the public institutions and business enterprises.

However, the efficacy of these national chapters is far from palpable. For any corruption measures to be successful, the government must show its eagerness to cooperate (Kuper 2004: 184). Similarly, influencing the corporate sector is an equally difficult task; on the contrary, this may lead to compromising effects on the work and reputation of social organizations working in this area, since the corporate sector is known to manipulate such collaborations primarily for publicity purposes, while resisting to change in its fraudulent business behaviors (Wang and Rosenau 2001: 25–49).

In the international corruption campaign, the International Initiative on Corruption and Governance (IICG) is a small radical group that has emerged in recent years. This organization has argued that the TI, both in its approach and practice, is tightly controlled by international financial institutions and powerful business groups. Accordingly, the ICCG calls for the need to launch a more autonomous and persuasive international campaign that would expose the global economic, business and political structures and systems of corruption, in addition to the national and localized practices of corruption.[12]

The World Social Forum

The WSF is nearly a synonym to describing today's alternative globalization movement. Its origin, progress and public impact have commonly been referred to in the national and international media and increasingly in academic discussions. The movement claims to be an open and unique worldwide political space for civil society groups to come together periodically to discuss negative consequences of the present neoliberal market economy and defects of the institutional political representation (i.e., its inability to adequately represent the public voice as well as avoid the dominance of the market forces over politics). We will come back in more details on the different facets of the movement in the third part of the book. At this stage, two specific points should be noted. Firstly, it is the first major international movement that has been able to maintain a strong foothold in the South (i.e., in addition to the North). Second, through its global social forums, it performs as an anchoring annual event among a significant number of social movements and organizations. As a matter of fact, the four international campaigns described above, despite a considerable divergence in their organizational compositions, objectives and goal orientations, regularly come together to this event.

Yet how the WSF operates internally as a movement is little known. What is the nature of its organizational set up, managerial culture and decision-making processes? How is leadership composed and how is national and regional representation to the movement organized? What are the inherent tensions with respect to the internal adaptation of political strategies and future direction of the movement? Evidently, many of these questions remain equally valid with regard to the four selected transnational campaigns outlined above.

In an effort to explain empirically these various organizational elements as well as their specific effects to internal power relations, we use two types of qualitative sources. First, four selected transnational campaigns will be examined in relation to their mobilization capacity. In particular, four national contexts (i.e., Argentina, Bolivia, Senegal and the Philippines) will be studied to understand how these campaigns are structured from international to national levels. The prime information and insights used here emanate from Grimson and Pereyra 2008a, Mayorga and Cordova 2008, Thioub and Diop 2007 and Tadem 2009a—a series of national reports produced under an international research project which the author earlier directed at the United Nations Research Institute for Social Development (UNRISD), Geneva.

Second, two principal sources of information are utilized to analyze the WSF case. A first source of the material used in this work is basically derived from the use of the WSF Internet site.[13] A second source includes the author's direct observations of three of its important forums: the European Social Forum, Paris, 2003; World Social Forum, Mumbai, 2004; and World Social Forum, Nairobi, 2007. These two sources of information are combined with the review of the available secondary literature in English and French languages.

ORGANIZATIONAL LIFE AND THE DIMENSION OF POWER

As can be imagined, the selected transnational campaigns and WSF do not possess exactly the same nature of internal organization life. This is primarily because these two categories of organizations differ somewhat in their articulation of the nature and degree of social transformations that should take place. For example, the WSF, as its foremost motto "another world is possible" suggests, likes to believe in long-term perspectives and far-reaching societal changes. Within the selected four transnational campaigns, the Attac movement is the only group that may appear close to sharing this vision. Then again, this movement is not completely uncompromising in that it seriously challenges the legitimacy of the public institutions such as the State. On the contrary, this organization seems to attach a great deal of importance to the continued existence and resilient role of the State in welfare provisioning and labor negotiations in the face of an increased encroachment from the market forces (Ancelovici 2002: 444–455). Regarding the question of an enhanced regulation of the market or imposing a small levy on currency transactions, the movement's demands remain fairly moderate and contained. In any event, it does not call for replacing the market economy altogether. Predictably, the debt relief, trade justice and anti-corruption campaigns, on their part, do not look for overthrowing the "system," even though in some cases they may be urging for substantial changes in their respective areas of intervention.

Once again, it should be noted that when the WSF began discussing "alternative proposals" in responding to the initial criticism that it remained weak in postulating concrete propositions (Teivainen 2001: 59), the movement found itself supporting mainly the more moderate "reformist" proposals such as debt relief, the removal of trade barriers by Northern countries, imposition of an international currency taxation, etc. This resulted in the WSF strongly espousing transnational campaigns, while, as already noted, most transnational campaigns were already supporting the movement. This kind of mutual sponsoring was also observed across such campaigns as human rights, women's movement, environmental activism and indigenous peoples' rights (Keck and Sikkink 1998: 9–10). Taken as a whole, within both groups, in order to be able to constantly maintain the desired nature of ideological elasticity and reciprocal engagement, an informal and adaptive way of functioning seemed most essential.

According to this line of reasoning, a greater collective identity should be constructed aiming primarily at opposing the existing "structure of power" (Dubet and Thaler 2004: 561–564). The notion of "power" construed here is therefore essentially that of an oppressive and extra-organizational phenomenon. As such, power is considered as an unwarranted outcome for a proficient running of the organization. It follows then that no powerful leaders or political parties should emerge to muster the organizational power. The assumption also goes that by allowing each and every participating organization to operate with a light administrative structure and develop and implement concrete actions in an informal and largely autonomous manner, not only such unwelcome processes of the appropriation of power may be avoided but also many practical solutions could be searched out and widely tested. This approach naturally rejects the need to have to take the State power through elections or revolutionary means to introduce major changes. The idea basically is to persist with localized and self-governing actions that will eventually change the society from inside without taking the power; and this process would thus symbolize ultimately "a step towards the abolition of power relations" (Holloway 2005: 17).

Nevertheless, to function as an international movement, a certain form or degree of organizational coordination transpires to be an unavoidable prerequisite. In particular, any attempt to operate in diverse local, national and regional contexts as well as make it increasingly visible worldwide implies that the movement must extend its outreach to a greater geographical space. A common way of doing this has often involved the structuring of organizational activities along a vertical line, in other words from the transnational to the national level. This has especially been the case with international campaigns, but the WSF, too, is not any exception to this rule. In both cases, many of the organizational statements, internal and external communications and calls for wider mobilizations are carried out by posting news articles, commentaries and persuasive editorials on the Internet, combined with the use of email messages and alerts and electronic newsletters; and these methods have progressively adapted new forms of communications such as the video conferences.

We will see that the organizational life that involves the coordination of activities between international and national level is not completely straightforward. There are many inherent tensions between a populist notion of power suggesting that every one within the movement should have equal decision-making potential and the realities of an organizational life that frequently pushes towards rapid decision making confined to few individuals or groups. But is there a clear trend in fashioning the organizational design as a manifest alibi to power holding? In any event, we shall observe that the organizational life of both constituents of alternative globalization movement (i.e., transnational campaigns and the WSF) included in the study largely evolve around careful maneuvering and collaboration.

The remaining structure of the book is as follows: part 2 discusses the experiences of transnational campaigns involving national dynamics in four selected countries. A detailed examination of the WSF is provided in part 3. Finally, part 4 will provide syntheses and conclusions.

NOTES

1. "No matter what certain hypocrites tell us, the power is the first of the pleasures."

2. (Stendhal 1959:125).

3. However, according to Clegg, the recent dominant models (i.e., developed frequently at business schools) "neglect power" and there was a need to "focus more realistically on power and its practice" in future organizational studies (Clegg 2002: 438; see also Clegg 1989).

4. He says, "The herdsmen therefore have authority over oxen, the stockbreeders of horses over the horses, and that all those which one calls animal-grazers are precisely viewed as the Masters of the animals of which they have the watch" (Xenophon 1967:25).

5. Crozier, for example, refers to the phenomenon of lower level technicians possessing a significant degree of clout in the production system through their newly acquired knowledge on the running of vital machineries and other types of savoir faire (Crozier 1963).

6. *Association pour la taxation des transactions financières et pour l'aide aux citoyens.*

7. DEF, http://www.weforum.org/pdf/SummaryReports/Davos_report.pdf; page 4 (accessed May 24, 2010).

8. See, for example: AGP (Peoples' Global Action). http://www.agp.org (accessed May 12, 2010); Alternative libertaire. http://www.alternativelibertaire.org (accessed May 12, 2010).

9. Also known as "ethical tribunals." A common feature of national social activism in most developing countries, these tribunals often invite legal and paralegal experts, as well as affected population groups, to critically assess the legitimacy and consequences of foreign debt. Organizers hold popular hearings and pronounce verdicts. Perceptibly, a common purpose of this action has been to highlight the general debt dilemmas in developing countries, since legally these judgements are binding to no one.

10. Focus on the Global South. http://www.focusweb.org/main/html (accessed May 12, 2010).

11. This membership is, however, based entirely on voluntary contributions, and all individuals, once registered, continue to be counted as being members, irrespective of whether they have been paying their dues or not (Attac. http://www.attac.org/spip.php?article.8206 (accessed May 12, 2010).

12. IICG (International Initiative on Corruption and Governance). http://www.peoplesgovernance.org (accessed May 12, 2010).

13. WSF. http://www.forumsocialmundial.rog.br (accessed March 15, 2010, among others).

II

FOUR TRANSNATIONAL CAMPAIGNS IN FOUR NATIONAL CONTEXTS

2

Transnational Campaigns and National Linkages

So far as the transnational campaigns that we have specifically chosen to assess—namely debt relief, trade justice, global taxation on currency transactions and anti-corruption movements—there are at least three reasons as to why these organizations require establishing linkages at the national level. First, basically their legitimacy is at stake. In an attempt to assert their "international" or "global" standing, it is obvious that these campaigns require to gain a wide public consent from the "trans-national" to the national level. As such, they must maintain national affiliate organizations, in addition to their international outfits. Furthermore, in order to avoid the risk of being criticized for a narrow representational base, they need to promote visibility of national groups (or at least a certain number of national key figures) within their organizational structures. Such legitimacy is fundamental to achieving approving recognition not only from the social actors and movements, but also from the public authorities and general citizens.

Second, despite increased international economic and cultural integrations in recent decades, the national setting continues to remain acutely important in contention politics. In any event, if citizens or their organizations are to press on with their claims and propositions, the nation State, by and large, is a prime arena for social dialogue. For instance, they can make use of the existing laws (both customary and modern); they can utilize the influence of political parties, local administrations, the national parliament, and so forth; they can employ methods of strikes and public demonstrations; they can obviously seek to influence the public opinion. In a nutshell, the State is both a visible and approachable protagonist. It is in this sense, Melucci affirms, that "the participation in collective action implies the affiliations to past networks" at the national level (Melucci 1996:

292). Indeed, according to della Porta, the current international activism is largely based on national organizations, including trade unions, leftist political parties, students' federations, women's organizations, environmental movements and charitable organizations (della Porta 2005: 10–26). Thus, the national context stands out to be an important resource for the mobilization efforts at the international level.

Third, and most crucially, international campaigns often vehicle ideas and propositions that have direct significance to the national setting. Whether it is the movement linked to debt relief, trade justice, international currency taxation or anti-corruption, they all formulate calls essentially in relation to the specific conditions prevalent in developing countries. In the event these campaigns fail to take on national character (in addition to international), the plain question that rises is: On whose behalf do they actually speak for? Logically, the arrival of activists from different countries would also lead to the enhanced popularization of the key demands or objects of protests advanced by these campaigns, as well as working out of certain localized solutions. Most vitally, as these campaigns desire to build up and intensify their advocacy activities, a growing numerical endorsement from the national and sub-national level is all but nearly obligatory.

So the related questions are: How are organizational links built between international and national actors? Who defines the agenda? How are tasks and the available resources distributed? How are important coordination and communication aspects handled? Above all, what are the specific interests of actors arising out of a national context in importing issues from international campaigns?

NATIONAL SIGNIFICANCE OF TRANSNATIONAL CAMPAIGNS IN ARGENTINA, BOLIVIA, SENEGAL AND THE PHILIPPINES

Before moving on to considering the national linkages of transnational campaigns, it is useful to briefly explore the socio-political and economic circumstances in four selected countries. The intent here is not merely to provide the reader with the minimum national context to comprehend the presence and profile of the mobilization of transnational campaigns, but also to help grasp how certain national dynamics may prove significant in the appropriation and expansion of certain thematic areas. Discernibly, plentiful differences exist among these four countries in terms of their historical evolution, legal and constitutional norms, political structures, and so forth. But there are two major similarities that have strongly shaped the scope, pattern and intensity of international and national activism experienced in recent years. First, to a varying degree, these countries have experienced tensions in their attempt to establish and consolidate a functional democracy. Second, ever since the 1980s, they have come under pressure to adhere to economic liberalization and austerity measures with considerable social and economic costs are being borne by ordinary citizens.

Argentina

Argentina is illustrative of both these political and economic tribulations and also in a very complex manner. On the one hand, unlike many Latin American countries, democracy was restored as early as 1983 with the protection of civil rights, including the holding of fair elections, and removal of the army from the political arena. The country's democratic tradition has also carried on despite major economic crises, as writes Levitsky:

> Argentine democracy survived a series of extraordinary tests, including the 1989-90 hyperinflationary crisis, the Menem government's radical economic reforms, and, most recently, the most severe depression in the country's history. Few Latin American democracies have survived such economic shocks. (Levitsky 2005: 63)

On the other hand, the ordinary citizens remained highly "skeptical about the political parties and other political institutions (including Congress and the courts)" (Epstein and Pion-Berlin 2006: 24). Some authors also note an important government policy ambiguity: for example, on the one side, it continued to articulate for a strong State intervention in social domains, and on the other, it increasingly privileged privatization, self-management and economic autonomy at the detriment of the essential institutional function (Svampa 2005: 118). By and large, the government's durability was built on its ability to manage and stabilize the national economy. In that sense, the formal or institutional politics tended to remain highly subservient to the economic policies or conditions.

Foweraker, Landman and Harvey suggest that it was actually the debt crisis that made the military regimes fall out of power in much of Latin America (Foweraker, Landman and Harvey 2003: 27). Argentina was certainly a strong example of this outcome since the military government could not sustain itself, among others, the steady buildup of a vast foreign debt between 1976 and 1981. While the military regime ended in 1983, the civil governments in the 1980s and 1990s continued to confront hyperinflation, fiscal deficits and massive foreign debt, causing acute political instabilities (Tedesco 1999: 174). In addition to this, the structural adjustment policies prescribed by international financial institutions as solutions to the economic crises facing the country resulted in speedy privatization and dismantling of the industrial sector and the retraction of the State in public services such as health care, educational provisioning and pension. This has had the consequences of provoking widespread social and

political agitations and the eventual pressure on the successive governments to quit very frequently (indeed, the country experienced the change
of five presidents in ten days in 2001).

In 1999, the country's foreign debt reached 145 billion USD; as such, it
proved to be increasingly difficult to recycle the outstanding debt by simply
borrowing additional funds (Epstein and Pion-Berlin 2006: 6). Between
2001 and the arrival of Kirchner to power in May 2003, an unprecedented
level of economic, social and political upheavals occurred, with the country's astounding debt affecting the Western financial markets and economic
growth. Subsequently, the new government managed to swiftly negotiate
more than 110 billion USD of debt with Western creditors and the IMF.[1]
Nevertheless, Argentina's foreign debt has continued to stay extraordinarily
high: some 128.2 billion USD in 2008.[2]

Likewise, corruption has remained an endemic problem in Argentina,
with wealthy politicians, business people, judges and high level government officials being involved in all sorts of fraudulent propensities: commission taking, shady business transactions including arms trade, the
embezzlement of public funds, etc. According to some scholars, this has
"profoundly de-legitimized Argentine politics" (Media 2006: 232). The
Transparency International Corruption Indices suggest that in 2009 Argentina ranked in the 106th position (out of a total number of 180 countries
included in the corruption ranking). What is especially noteworthy is that
between 2001 and 2009, the country dropped from the 57th to the 106th
position,[3] meaning that the country's reputation significantly depreciated
from the pick period of the economic crisis in 2001 to more recent years.

Some authors believe that, with the deepening of the economic crises,
corruption gradually descended (or extended) to the provincial level. Here
corruption touched not only at the level of distribution of public housing
and land, federal funds, public works budget and pension funds, but also
at a level as low as "soup kitchens serving poor neighborhoods" (Auyero
2001: 38). It has been argued that widespread corruption was in fact a key
cause for frequent popular riots in certain regions (ibid. 39).

Given a heavy socio-economic and political cost of foreign debt, unstable
financial markets and corruption, the arguments for a firm control of the financial criminality, capital flight and money laundering, on the one hand,
and the taxing of financial operations for social welfare programs, on the
other, tended to receive a frequent echo in the public opinion as well as
political circles. Accordingly, it is not surprising that the Argentina Attac
branch was established in 1999—that is, within a year of the conception of
the Attac international movement in France.

The issue of trade liberalization was an area around which Attac Argentina, as well as many other social organizations including trade unions
could unite without any great difficulty. Enhanced trade liberalization

was the remedy for the country's economic ills frequently prescribed by the leading financial institutions, in addition to structural adjustments on urban wages and public spending. The core logic behind this was that, since Argentina's external trade involving agriculture and manufacturing goods represented a significant part of its GDP (i.e., 24.5 percent in 2008[4]), the country stood to make considerable gains through expansion in regional and international trade. Yet before any such gains could occur, the government was obliged to reduce tariffs and trade barriers as required by the WTO regulations and within the context of constructing the Mercosur. In this regard, the Free Trade Area of the Americas (FTAA) treaty was considered to be a particularly disquieting new evolution (further details below).

In any event, since the country's major economic crises unfolded together with the discussions on trade liberalization, the topic suddenly attracted a lot of debates within the Argentinean civil society. The FTAA initiative, in specific, was believed to be a latest United States stratagem to promote its political and economic interests in the region. This view was also largely shared by the political elites of many Latin American countries, including Brazil and Argentina (Franco 2007: 276). In contrast, the market in the United States was seen generally small and restricted to Argentinean products, as compared especially to the European Union or Mercosur. On the whole, the reinforcement of regional trade within the framework of the Mercosur was considered to be particularly advantageous to the country's economy, as well as boosting the general negotiating capacity of the regional bloc (i.e., the Mercosur) vis-à-vis the United States, European Union, WTO and Asian countries (Rapoport 2003: 119).

Bolivia

Bolivia is one of the poorest countries in Latin America. It has also one of the worst patterns of income inequality in the region. Indeed, in 2007, the poorest 20 percent of the population shared only 2.7 percent of income, whereas the top 20 percent enjoyed as much as 61.2 percent of income.[5] This disparity often goes together with the ethnic origin. The country has the largest national proportion of the indigenous populations in Latin America (constituting nearly 60 percent of the total population). At the same time, the majority of the population is economically poor and politically powerless. These factors have cumulatively led to the production of a great deal of social tensions, with the Bolivian State trying to accommodate certain demands in the past (e.g., through improved land entitlements and increased political representation of the indigenous peoples). The period between 1982 and 2003 was characterized by a degree of political stability through social pacts between diverse political parties and groups, but during this period institutional measures also marked a clear shift to-wards a more liberal market-centered economic approach (Mayorga 2005: 150–151).

The ability to maintain political stability and embrace liberal economy policies at times helped Bolivia to acquire approval from Western countries and donor agencies. For example, the country attained the status of a heav-ily indebted poor country (HIPC). In 1998, it secured debt relief worth 2 billion USD, thereby reducing its external debt nearly by half (Franco, 2007: 101). Nevertheless, its inability to repay the remaining half meant that the country was obliged to continue to borrow new funds, and by 2008 its external debt amounted 5.5 billion USD.[6]

As part of its international image building, during 1982–2003, Bolivia signed several international conventions on corruption and attempted to implement many of the initiatives promoted by international agencies such as the Organization of American States, World Bank, United Nations and OECD. Domestically, too, corruption was considered generally harm-ful for a sound running of development activities. However, much of this recognition was limited to the declaration of intents. The country has been persistently classified among the worst corrupt countries in the world in the Transparency International Corruption Indices (120th position in 2009). The main issue regularly brought up by the TI included the collusion be-tween the State functionaries and private sector, because the law allows the latter to hire former government employees. Besides, the judiciary system has been known to be particularly fraudulent.[7]

Unlike in Argentina, the issues of market volatilities, currency specula-tion, tax havens and their consequences to the national economy were never considered pertinent in Bolivia. Even though the Argentina case was a frequent point of reference, no specific public debate could crystallize in this area. This is primarily because during this time the public opinion and principal social movements were primarily concerned with the fundamen-tal question of how to achieve an effective national sovereignty over the use of its natural resources and construe the effects of the continental and international trade liberalization treaties, rather than to explore a narrow proposal of a currency transaction tax as such.

By this time, it was generally recognized that the national politics and economic liberalization measures had "failed to deliver better living con-ditions to the poor and excluded" (Mayorga 2005: 172). This was indeed so despite the fact that significant debt relief measures had taken place. In the meantime, Bolivia's internal market was swiftly opened for foreign investment. The irony was that in more recent years, the country's GDP growth rate has remained fairly strong (4.2 percent in 2004 to 6.1 percent in 2008[8]). Furthermore, there was an important discovery and growing exploitation of oil and gas. Instead the attempt to increase productivity and efficiency resulted in the massive firings of workers in the State-owned sectors, namely mining and railroads. At the same time, the demand for Bolivian labor shrunk in Argentina because of its successive economic crises in the late 1990s and early 2000s. In order to reduce fiscal deficits, the government, following the advice from the IMF, sought to raise new taxes on hydrocarbon products. However, these policy measures provoked a widespread popular discontentment, especially in urban centers. The conflict is commonly described as the "tax war" (see on this Kohl and Farthing 2006: 111–116).

Another major social upheaval that country saw during 2000 and 2002 was the "water war" in the Cochabamba area. This event was intimately linked to the consequences of the privatization of public utilities and rise of prices stating the logic of financial equilibriums. A major turning point in this was that a multinational consortium which bought the city's water exploitation contract looked to have an exclusive right not only over the urban drinking water system, but also over ground water (including wells), surface irrigation systems, and rainwater catchments (ibid. 164). It should be recalled that all these urban tensions were occurring in a background of a persistent economic marginalization of the vast majority of the rural population. In particular, with the US pressure to eradicate coca cultivation without sufficiently offering viable alternatives had led many rural households to deny an important source of their customary livelihood.

In short, these different social outcomes were to unfold in successive turbulences and political crises leading to the January 2006 election of Evo Morales (a trade union activist representing the politically excluded coca-growing Aymara indigenous community) as the country's president. Soon after his election victory, Morales followed a distinctly defiant political line, as we shall observe afterwards. In general, social and political problems had tended to give support to more discursive and radical views throughout the early 2000s. Not only the legitimacy of the institutions such as the IMF and World Bank were critically questioned, but also the reforms and negotiations carried out by the previous governments on foreign debt and trade regimes came under acute public scrutiny. With particular respect to the issue of trade regimes, albeit the preceding governments generally remained keen to ratify, the trade treaty under the FTAA negotiations took several years, and from 2000 onwards the national as well as South American regional atmosphere (cf. the Argentinean financial crises and arrival of left-lenient presidents in Brazil, Argentina and Venezuela) became highly suspicious for concluding any specific trade deals with the United States. Furthermore, very much like in Argentina, the expansion in regional trade relations was considered more gainful to the country by the new political elites, as well as by most social movements.[9]

What is significant in the case of Bolivia was the emphatic support of the Evo Morales's government to open out alternative forms of trading relations. One such scheme has been the "Peoples Trade Treaty" (*Tratado de Commercio de los Pueblos*) among politically likeminded neighbouring socialist countries. This may represent an attractive niche market for certain population groups, since regional tastes and demands can considerably vary with that of international ones. For example, under the recent agreement with Venezuela and Cuba, Bolivia has attempted to develop and export industrial milk, tea, oleaginous and wood products, among others (Mayorga and Cordova 2008: 25). Manifestly, these are not the usual sorts of products sought after in the international market. However, the country's vast internal distance with a poor road infrastructure and particularly its long distance to the nearest sea is that the expansion in trading activities remains highly problematical for Bolivia.

Senegal

Even if a single socialist party ruled Senegal for 40 years, the country has avoided the stigma of a repressive regime that characterized many African nations. A certain degree of press freedom, intellectual activities and labor and civic movements was continually preserved; and since the early 1980s, the opposition political parties regularly contested elections, with key leaders frequently joining the national unity government as cabinet ministers during the 1990s. Following the 2000 presidential election, a center-right Senegalese Democratic Party, led by Abdoulaya Wade, came to power with a pledge to swiftly open and liberalize the national economy (Galvan 2001: 52–54).

Undeniably a poor country, national income distribution patterns in Senegal have remained relatively better than all the other three countries included in this study (with the poorest 20 percent of the population sharing 6.2 percent of income in 2005[10]). Within its socialist political tradition, the government directed by Léopold Senghor until 1981 and his successor Abdou Diouf throughout the 1980s sought to represent the broad interests of the impoverished yet majority rural population. Since the 1980s, a high reliance on the ground nuts economy and the failure of the industrial sector to grow, on the one hand, and the declining commodity price for ground nuts in the international market, successive droughts and a rapid urbanization process (in large part due to rural exodus with a high expectation for urban employment and better living conditions), on the other, forced the government to have to seek advice and assistance from the leading financial institutions, notably the World Bank and IMF. Consequently, common to many African countries, Senegal underwent major structural adjustment programs (SAPs). These programs have had the general effect of speedily deregulating and liberalizing the national economy. They have also had the effect of reducing the welfare spending across the board.

At the same time, the government was obliged to borrow additional resources to finance the poverty reduction projects, as well as make the general economic activities get going. The irony was that much of this additional borrowing was concluded with the same lending agencies that were supposed to assist the country for a sound economic development policy in the first place, with the World Bank group representing 64 percent of the country's total debt by the end of 2007.[11] Like Bolivia, as we saw above, Senegal was included in the group of countries classified as Heavily Indebted Poor Countries, thereby allowing the country to benefit from important debt relief measures. At the same time, since new loans had to be taken in order to pay the remaining debt, the total sum of foreign debt continued to stay quite substantial: 2.8 billion USD in 2008.[12] Moreover, the reduction and new allocations of debt were associated with stringent conditionalities imposed by the leading financial institutions and Western governments.

One such conditionality was precisely the liberalization and opening up of the national economy for an unobstructed external investment and international trading. Foreign donors and the government perceived this to be "the only solution to reinforce the growth and development of the Senegalese economy" (Daffé 2002: 79). Yet the country's attempts to reintegrate in the world market has not produced any satisfactory results, owing primarily to the lack of articulation between agriculture and industry, weak diversification in the manufacturing sector and impediments in import substitution measures involving consumer products in urban areas (ibid.). A sizeable and continued decline in the international trade of ground nuts (the country's main export item) has particularly been disquieting. In 2008, the export earnings from agriculture as a whole constituted only 25 percent of the GDP,[13] in large part due to the reduction in the international commodity prices and to a lesser extent imposition of complex quality norms and deliberate price cuts of similar products coming from major economies like the European Union and the United States. In the meantime, due to price fluctuations and market competitions, the diversification of production in cotton, rice, fruits, vegetables and poultry have also shown no promising results. Given this gloomy economic performance, certain authors saw the country harboring basically a "sterile democracy" (Sidibé 2006: 130), implying that a free electoral system could not accompany stable economic growth and redistribution.

Trade unions, NGOs and social movements believed that the prevailing trading systems needed to be changed if peasants and artisans were to ameliorate their livelihood conditions. The Senegalese products should find an improved access to the world market. In particular, producers representing the agricultural, artisanal and textile sectors should have a minimum amount of secured revenue. Very much like in Argentina and Bolivia, owing to the unfair nature of international trade, an enhanced regional integration was considered increasingly a more viable trading option. For this reason, urban consumers were urged to display citizen's concern by privileging the consumption of local and regional products (albeit little success). At a more practical level, different ideas were evoked in terms of how quality control measures could be reinforced to meet international standards, with the ultimate goal of facilitating the increased exportation of Senegalese products.

As for the issue of international taxation or Tobin Tax, the topic received a certain degree of political attention in the country, including discussions at the national parliament. Luckily, the country avoided the wrath of financial crises experienced in many developing countries in the recent past. Nevertheless, these crises tended to indirectly impact upon the Senegalese national economy through the weakening of its currency, falling international market prices of raw materials and lowering of export earnings. For a small and weak economy like that of Senegal, the prime interest in the international taxation proposition has been the potential of obtaining additional external funds for activities related to social welfare and development projects through this mechanism. This explained why the Senegalese government remained so enthusiastic on initiatives involving the passenger tax on airplane tickets introduced in a number of countries.

In this regard, it should also be noted that, a sizeable quantity of capital has tended to continually leave the country. For example, between 1995 and 2003 foreign direct investment in Senegal amounted to 712 million USD, and out of this, 514 million USD was repatriated as profits (UNCTAD 2005: 86). Arguably, hence, if short-term capital movements were subjected to regulation and control mechanisms like the Tobin tax, there would have been a potential for retaining some of the capital entries, as well as the profits that were commonly repatriated. This would have naturally financed imports as well as encouraged more durable production and investment activities.

Finally, with regard to the issue of corruption, Senegal has been relatively well-placed in the IT's corruption chart (e.g., the 99th place in 2009). Nevertheless, its recent corruption record suggests a steadily deteriorating situation—the country was downgraded from 71st in 2007 to 99th in 2009.[14] Without a doubt, corruption has been a widespread phenomenon in the country. Some authors argue that corruption has a cultural trait in that what is considered legally perverse does not always constitute culturally reprehensible offense (Sidibé 2006: 150). Others prefer to insist that all forms of corruption are blameworthy (Chabal and Daloz 1999: 122–123). Yet both strands commonly join to reprove administrative, political and economic forms of corruptions, especially involving the State apparatus and large business enterprises.

Indeed, denouncing of corruption has not only been the preoccupation of the academics, journalists and human rights activists, but also of different political parties. Nor have they lacked legal instruments to be applied. Senegal, for example, has signed most of the international anti-corruption conventions and enacted many essential national laws. The fundamental problem has been the lack of their effective implementation and follow-up. In particular, the successive governments have failed to mobilize public opinion or civil society at large around the widespread phenomenon of corruption. Besides, public resources continue to represent the primary sources of funding for political parties. At times, according to certain authors, corruption control measures have been used simply to harass political opponents (Hadjadj 2002: 32).

The Philippines

Past political developments have largely conditioned many of the recurrent debates on foreign debt, trade or corruption in the Philippines. These developments comprised the (a) the martial law period related to the Marcos regime (1972–1986), (b) transition from authoritarianism to democracy, (c) emergence of neoliberalism as the dominant paradigm as exemplified by globalization, (d) 1997 Asian financial crisis, and (e) persistence of patronage politics and corruption within State apparatus (Tadem 2009b: 8–9).

The debate on the debt issue, for example, already surfaced during the Marcos administration and has continued to stay in the public domain ever since. During the Marcos period, the prime rational for opting to borrow external loans was to boost the national industrialization process through export promotion. As this did not materialize as anticipated, the regime confronted a high fiscal deficit and was pushed into continually borrowing. In addition to this, a considerable amount of externally negotiated financial resources was lost through fraud. Some authors have asserted that "debt-driven" policy was Marco's fitting strategy to extract enormous quantities of funds from international financial institutions, bilateral donors and commercial banks (de Dios and Hutchcroft 2003: 49). When the regime came to an end in 1986, the country's total external debt amounted to 27.2 billion USD.

Yet with the advent of democracy and the arrival of Aquino to power, foreign debt continued to increase. Contrary to common expectations, she pledged to meet foreign debt obligations in order to "regain the confidence of investors and creditors as soon as possible" (Balisacan and Hill 2003: 51). Her "decision in favor of full debt repayment and IMF conditionality meant that technocrats rather than social reformists set the economic agenda in the new government" (Abinales and Amoroso 2005: 233). In 2004, the country's debt stood at 60.9 billion USD and by 2008 it reached 64.8 billion USD[15] (ironically considerably more than the Marcos era). Worse yet, not considered to be among the very poor countries, the Philippines did not qualify as a Heavily Indebted Poor Country, and as such, it could not benefit from international debt relief measures under this scheme.

Corruption is another domain of public debate in the Philippines, and this has remained so during much of the past three decades. Undeniably, much of the popular opposition to the Marcos regime had surfaced around the incident of a widespread corruption. According to Kang, "Excessive power concentrated in the hands of political elites and their cronies led to a state-dominated economy permeated by large patronage and corruption" (Kang 2002: 190). This assertion seemed to generally hold even for the post-Marcos democratic period. For example, Estrada (the third president after the fall of Marcos) was charged by the Congress in January 2001 with "bribery, grafts, and corrupt practices," among others (Hedman 2006: 2).

Certain authors have also sought to explain corruption as the prime cause for the 1997 financial crisis (Corsetti 1999: 1211–1236). Overall, it is agreed that corruption has been "one of the most important variables for growth" as "Philippine governmental policies always remained subject to manipulation" (Kang ibid.185 and 10, respectively). The available information suggests that the magnitude of corruption has continued to accrue, and this seems to be the case irrespective of the foundation of a more democratic system. As a matter of fact, the Philippines jumped from the 66th most corrupt country in 2001 to the 139th place in 2009.[16]

Appeals for democracy and the electoral transparency came together with reflections on how to achieve economic development satisfying local livelihoods, especially in the predominant agricultural sector. In this vein, various community trading schemes were created from the 1970s onwards, and these schemes multiplied in later decades. Northern Churches, NGOs, consumer cooperatives and development agencies assisted in establishing various business cooperatives promoting crafts and agricultural products. These initiatives were seen as crucial not only for reinforcing economic welfare activities at the local level, but also for the national economy as a whole through export earnings. However, any significant expansion in such projects was ultimately linked to the accessibility of Northern markets, including the need to understand and follow many complex trading and market conditions. For example, the community trade project supported by the Oxfam Great Britain was shut down due to a declining demand of Philippine handicrafts in Europe, owing apparently to a growing international competition (Cabilo 2009: 149–150).

A great deal of debate has occurred particularly around the consequences of trade liberalization. In the past two decades, the country's declared ambition was to fully integrate itself to the regional economic body ASEAN (Association of South-East Asia Nations) as well as to a lesser extent to APEC (Asia Pacific Economic Cooperation). In more recent years, its ambitions have evolved around the attempt to obtain a full membership in the WTO and actively participating in international trade negotiations. This has in turn implied the lowering of national tariffs, lifting of import restrictions and opening up of previously restricted sectors and industries to foreign ownership. Trade liberalization was in general believed to create employment and economic growth. Yet even the orthodox authors associated with the World Bank have believed that "actual employment and export growth did not come anywhere near the vision that supporters of the trade liberalization painted during the debates that eventually led the Philippine senate to ratify the membership of the Philippines in the World Trade Organization" (Medalla 2007: 213). On the other hand, the more critical authors have argued that the government's trade liberalization was "achieved at the cost of multiple bankruptcies and massive job losses. The loss of industrial casualties included paper products, textiles, ceramics, rubber products, furniture and fixtures, petrochemicals, beverage, wood, shoes, petroleum oils, clothing accessories, and leather goods" (Bello, Docena, de Guzman and Laig 2004: 24–25; see also Wui and Tadem 2006 on the impacts of trade liberalization affecting vegetable production, garment and hog industries).

Lastly, the 1997 financial crisis leading to a massive devaluation of the Philippine peso, capital flight, and weakening of the banking system bestowed a great deal of support to the critics of the liberal economic model. At the same time, the debate concerning specifically the proposition of the currency taxation or Tobin Tax occurred in a very sporadic manner. No doubt many Filipino intellectuals pondered around the various prospects of responding to the volatility of financial and capital markets. But in general many of them tended to favor the idea of a flexible exchange rate, improving of corporate governance and imposing of prudent banking regulations (Lamberte 1999:15–18). A currency taxation proposition was considered a viable option only when all countries followed the initiative (Kim 2003:147–149). Nonetheless, like in the other three selected countries, an echo of the international currency transaction tax campaign began to surface in the Philippines, too. Notably similar to many developed as well as developing countries, a number of parliamentarians took interest in taking up the issue. The principal outcome of this initiative was the creation of a Congressional Planning and Budget Office, with the release of a paper calling for the imposition of a transaction tax for withdrawals, savings, current and term accounts (Molmisa 2009: 115).

In nutshell, we can say that, with varying degrees, each one of the four themes seemed to have occupied a certain place in the public life and institutional policy choice in all case study countries. The problem of debt stood out to be particularly noteworthy. It has been an important cause of the recent political upheavals in Argentina. In Bolivia, despite the fact that the country benefited from significant debt relief measures, the overall debt burden has continued to persist (owing to the need to borrow additional money to repay the remaining debt, as outlined above). This has also been more or less the same in Senegal. In the Philippines, too, the debt problem has tended to amplify, in part because the country was excluded from debt relief measures applied to the poorest nations.

Corruption appeared to be a widespread phenomenon in all national contexts. This has prompted international financial and development agencies to implement numerous anti-corruption projects. Likewise, corruption has stood out to be a matter of common and recurring concern among a vast number of formal institutions as well as political and civil society actors at the national level (further details on this latter category of actors will be given in the subsequent section).

In the same fashion, trade liberalization issues have keenly been debated in all four countries. In line with the recommendations from the WTO and international financial institutions and with the hope of achieving higher economic growth through international trade, the governments in these countries have unfailingly promoted trade liberalization. Yet the perceived benefits of trade for developing countries has been a matter of deep controversy, in part because various types of subsidies and trade barriers have continued to persist in the developed world, thus deterring the entry of Third World products while its accumulated past mercantilist experience and dominant economic, technological and political position invariably allow it to have the upper hand in reaping a good deal of the new worldwide trade benefits that arise.

Finally, currency speculation and financial instability are no longer an unfamiliar topic in these four countries. This has become an important theme for public debate not only in countries like Argentina and the Philippines, which have experienced acute volatility in national and regional financial markets, but also in smaller national economies such as Bolivia and Senegal. Indeed, regardless of the size of their economy, currency speculations and financial fluctuations have tended to severely affect prospects for short and long-term economic investment, employment creation and welfare provisioning. Nevertheless these implications have been stressed mainly within a narrow circle of economists with considerable difficulties in mobilizing common citizens and social organizations around this issue (further details in the following section).

It should thus be obvious that, in each of the national context, the themes of debt relief, corruption control, trade liberalization as well as financial and market volatility are more and more common features, at times triggering off considerable economic, social and political consequences. As a result of this, it is not surprising that various forms of collective debates and contestations would emerge. This also suggests a generalized scope for expanding transnational campaigns, since the existence of prior history, public interest and the mobilization efforts by certain actors at the national level should no doubt help them to broaden links and popularize their core problematic. Nevertheless, how do international campaigns in reality make their way into the national settings?

STRUCTURES AND MODUS OPERANDI OF
TRANSNATIONAL CAMPAIGNS IN NATIONAL CONTEXTS

According to Tarrow and McAdam, the expansion in transnational movements depends essentially on the "attribution of similarity" (existence of similar groups), "emulation" (similar actions) and in particular prospects of greater "diffusion" (transfer of information to previously established lines of interaction) and "brokerage" (transfer of information to formerly unconnected people or groups) (Tarrow and McAdam 2005: 126–128). Focusing on the civil rights and nuclear freeze movements in the United States and the Zapatista insurgency in Mexico, they examine how local contentions extend to other localities as a result of the successful diffusion of information on the initial action reaching broader areas, including its upward international influence. In this work, we are more interested in looking at the downward connection of international campaigns to national social dynamics. The broad notion of similarities in group formation, actions and the possibility of sharing information is a useful pointer to the understanding of scale shift of movements both upward and downward. However, we believe such a conception of resemblance must also take into account the varying degree of interests and influence that invariably get expressed in different spaces and scales of action.

Mindful of this problematic, in this section we propose to examine the structures and modus operandi of transnational campaigns as they seek to stretch out to the national level. In other words, how is overall organizational setup conceived in their effort to translate international initiatives into action at the national level? What is the relationship between the "headquarter" and national "divisions"? To be more precise, are the linkages between the center and subunits built on equal footing with regard to each others' autonomy, choice and specificity yet working together in areas of common interest? The composition and functioning of transnational campaigns are discussed below by considering successively each of the four national contexts.

Debt Relief Movement

A growing international connection occurred around the debt advocacy in Argentina following the 2001 financial and social crisis. The country's vast debt was, however, an important issue of public concern already in the 1980s, with certain political parties, labor unions and human rights organizations stating that the debt accumulated by the previous military regime was mostly illegitimate because of the lack of transparency in debt transactions, as well as its general mismanagement of the economy. Argentinean activists began to regularly participate in regional meetings around the debt question organized by trade unions and church organizations, including a major Continental Conference on Debt held in Cuba in 1985. But it was the creation of Dialogue 2000 (*Dialogo 2000*) in 1997 that national and international interactions on the Argentinean debt problem began to develop more intensively.

Established with the prime initiative of the Argentinean Nobel laureate Adolfo Pérez Esquivel and joined by the Mothers of the Plaza de Mayo (*Madres de Plaza de Mayo*[17]), Dialogue 2000 was heavily dominated by church-based associations. This was predictable given that during this time important regional and international preparations were taking place for the celebration of the Jubilee 2000, in line with the call by Pope Jean Paul II. The Bicameral Commission for Jubilee 2000 organized a series of public meetings on the country's debt predicament. In addition to this, it attempted to hold "ethical tribunals" on the issue of foreign debt and austerity measures that were followed, drawing on the regional experience of the Andean Tribunal on Foreign Debt in 1998. While these sorts of moral arguments and practical experimentations were certainly very important for Dialogue 2000, it attempted to particularly highlight the broader political and economic arguments for annulling debt, namely, the growing problem of unemployment and poverty due to the requirement to have to divert important resources for debt repayment, including a rapid shrinking of the country's middle class (Rivkin 2008: 164–177). Since Dialogue 2000 had already begun to work on such areas as the raising of public awareness and holding of public meetings on debt, the organization stood to be a natural candidate for closely working with this Commission.

The organization thus attempted to become an integral part of the ongoing social mobilization process linked in particular to the 2001 crisis. According to certain authors, the organized mobilization that took place around the debt problematic during this time was not at all futile, as it provided, among others, the national political authority with a strong social backing for not paying all the outstanding foreign debt unreservedly (Almeyra 2006: 202). Internationally, both the Jubilee 2000 and the Jubilee South greeted Dialogue 2000 with considerable esteem. But owing to its radical demand for repudiating all foreign debts, its affinity steadily grew with the Jubilee South. This latter organization on its part frequently brought allies from different continents to share information and insights on the debt crisis, particularly concerning the issue of Third-World debt incurred during the dictatorship. Dialogue 2000 became a full formal member of the Jubilee South's International Coordination Committee representing the Latin American and Caribbean region; and in recent years it has continued to play an active role in national as well as regional debt campaigns.

In Bolivia, the Catholic Church was the prime architect behind the mobilization of public opinion and certain sections of the State machinery around the debt issue. It did this with the advocacy ideas and financial resources coming from its counterparts in the Northern countries. By the time the international Jubilee 2000 was gearing up for the millennium celebration, the Bolivian Catholic Church managed to set up an important program on debt, titled "Yes to Life, No to Debt." Evidently the prime aim of this program was to exemplify the moral dimension of human sufferings associated with the debt burden. It collected 400,000 signatures in favor of its campaign. It has been suggested that this "was a significant factor for the final inclusion of Bolivia in the HIPC II during the G7 meeting that took place in Kohl, Germany" (in June 1999) (Mayorga and Cordova 2008: 18). This initiative was closely conducted in collaboration with Caritas and two German archdioceses, namely, the latter organizations providing the Bolivian campaigners with essential funds, insights on the functioning of the G7, as well as useful contacts in Germany on essential logistical matters.

By 2000, Bolivia experienced considerable debt relief measures. The government attempted to redirect some of the newly available resources to the poverty alleviation projects and to improving the production capacity in agriculture. These policies proved generally appealing to international NGOs and development agencies. The national Church hence gained credibility and consideration for its action. It also mobilized its local dioceses and exerted influence on the national media. One direct outcome of this was the setting up of the Jubilee Foundation (*Jubileo Fundación*) in 2003 under its leadership, with financial support coming from various German church orders. The primary objectives of this foundation were to gather vital information on the consequences of debt, mount awareness-raising campaigns and work as a prime civil society platform against poverty, particularly in relation to the achieving of national Millennium Development Goals (MDG).

However, with several important regional events taking place (e.g., the organization of a major WSF meeting, establishment of the continental Jubilee South office in the region, unfolding of popular mobilizations claiming effective national control over the exploitation of natural resources, namely, hydrocarbon products, or against the privatization of basic public utilities like water), a more radical stance calling for a complete cancellation of foreign debt began to occupy central position within the Foundation. This stance rejected the various conditions imposed by the leading financial institutions and debt-pardoning Western nations. Furthermore, there was an attempt to link the issue of debt with the larger problematic of trade liberalization, similar to Argentina. In the meantime, Evo Morales, who held very similar views on many these topics, got elected as the country's president. Naturally, this evolution has opened up a great many prospects for close collaboration between civil society organizations and formal institutional actors.

In Senegal, the international networks like the Jubilee 2000, Attac, Committee for the Abolition of Third World Debt (Cadtm[18]) and numerous Northern NGOs have been actively engaged around the debt problem for over a decade. The negotiation process involving the country's eventual inclusion in the HIPC initiative in 2000 created considerable scope for advocacy among national NGOs and social movements. The accompanied formal debt relief measures turned out to be a subject of severe critique though. There were chiefly three reasons for this: first, the debt repayment based on the calculation of economic growth was considered generally unrealistic; second, the multilateral agencies associated with debt relief measures frequently pushed for new loans; and third, the country's inclusion in the HIPC scheme was conditional to its implementation of further programs on privatization and trade liberalization (Dembele 2003: 16–17). During about the same time (i.e., December 2000), a major conference was organized in Dakar on the consequences of debt and structural adjustment policies in Africa. This event marked the final stage of the continent's mobilization for celebrating the Jubilee 2000 event at the international level. This also marked the radicalization of the national and regional debt activism with the prime assertion that enough debt had already been paid by poor African countries, and as such, there should be a total and unmitigated cancellation of the remaining debt.

Over the past decade, the foreign debt issue has been taken up by three principal social networks, although with a varying mobilization capacity. The Forum for African Alternatives operated as the formal national representative of the Jubilee South, but its advocacy activities have significantly declined in recent years. The Council of NGOs for Development Support (CONGAD[19]), an umbrella body of national NGOs, was another important network on debt campaign. In addition to its own activities on debt campaign, it hosted the headquarters of a regional NGO network: National Platforms of West and Central African NGOs (REPAOC[20]), with the mandate to work, among other aspects, on debt and other burning development questions in the region. The third group was composed of trade unions, specifically the National Union Independent Trade Union of Senegal (UNSAS[21]). All three networks commonly disseminated information on the nature and consequences of the country's debt dilemma, as well as organized mobilization campaigns, joining often forces collectively. One such mobilization was the conception and regular organization of the Senegalese Social Forum (FSS[22]).

Above and beyond, being an active member of the FSS, each of these three networks called for a radical overhaul in the economic policies imposed by the leading international financial institutions in the region. They persistently argued for ending the structural adjustment programs and increasing investment in social welfare with a strong intervention role for the State. As for the specific matter of debt, all three stood for a complete cancellation of debt. Nevertheless, in practice many of their member organizations commonly cooperated with the government and donor agencies in implementing the national chapter of the HIPC scheme (which was thus based only on the partial annulment of debt).

In the Philippines, the debt problem was articulated in relation to the Marcos autocratic regime and its misuses of loans, including many dire consequences on the material suffering of the bulk of the population. This standpoint began to attract international attention and collaboration from political and professional organizations (communist and socialist internationals, trade unions, etc.) and Christian charity foundations. This external support was fundamental for organizing workshops, forums and publication activities to censure the regime, as well as galvanize activists. This marked the first phase of the international connections around the debt question.

The second phase corresponded to the final years of the Marcos regime and the advent of democracy. This period saw a huge international connectivity. First, a major anti-debt movement the Freedom for Debt Coalition (FDC) was formally established in 1988. This movement, although dominated by forces from the left, sought to represent a wide spectrum of political organizations, including the business, churches and regional representations. While its main initial call was related to the total repudiation of fraudulent debts contracted under the Marcos regime, it gradually commenced to frame its activities around more pragmatic interventions. This is because the new democratic Aquino government agreed to honor the past loans in order to create a favorable business and investment atmosphere in the country. The movement with the care to become a useful ally to the government purposely avoided taking a confrontational line. In particular, it appealed for a (a) moratorium on debt payments until the country's capacity to pay; (b) policy to disengage with loans that were particularly associated with frauds; and (c) ceiling of debt payments at the level of 10 percent of the country's export earnings (Ariate and Molmisa 2009: 34).

These measured propositions obviously left a great deal of room for collaboration with the government, bilateral donor agencies and international financial institutions.

It was during this time that the Jubilee 2000 was being unveiled at the international level. To this and many other associated transnational campaigners, the FDC revealed to be a sturdy national movement. Furthermore, its call to repudiate fraudulent debts contracted under authoritarian and corrupt regimes was seen to be a pertinent experience to many other developing countries. This led the FDC to benefit from various regional and international civil society networks in accessing useful contacts and resources.

The third phase began in 1997, characterized by a general stagnation in the national debt relief movement. Overall, the FDC failed to influence the government to implement its key proposals. At the same time, the organization was not engaged in developing and implementing any specific debt-related projects. Beginning as an issue of political mobilization, debt slowly turned into a technical, economic matter to be handled mainly by government economists and the finance ministry. In the meantime, the Jubilee 2000 movement broke up into the Northern and Southern lines, with the latter arguing for a complete repudiation of debt and without any conditionality as per the initial advocacy of the FDC. However, this militant view was neither the taste of the major charity bodies nor the Northern institutional donor agencies. Likewise, as the country was not included in international financing projects for the poorest nations like the HIPC, the organization could not tap into the resources available from these schemes (i.e., through engagements with the government and donor agencies).

Meanwhile, the movement was progressively transformed into a large professional NGO with a sizeable headquarter, an international unit dealing with global campaigns and donor agencies, regional offices and the work programs spreading onto such domains as advocacy, research, media lobby and publications, thereby requiring a substantial income. At the same time, practically all of the FDC's funds came from international sources. This made the organization abandon its exclusive focus on debt and take on fiscal, monitory, privatization, industry regulation, trade and finance, labor, gender and environment issues. It even went onto proposing to change its very name (ibid. 43–44). All this obviously did not occur without internal debates and divisions. The ultimate result was the weakening role of the movement in debt campaign.

Campaign against Trade Liberalization

According to Grimson and Pereyra, the debate on the effects of eliminating tariffs and opening the economy to foreign capital in the public sector had already begun in Argentina in the 1970s (Grimson and Pereyra, 2008b:

31). Yet it was actually the creation and expansion of regional trade blocs, notably the FTAA, that gave the prime stimuli to national social mobilization. In April 2002, a dynamic coalition called the Self-Convoked No to the FTAA, No to Debt, No to Militarization and No to Poverty (*La Autoconvocatoria No al ALCA, No a la Deuda, No a la militarización y No a la Pobreza*) was conceived. An initial mobilization committee against the FTAA had already been established in 2001 at the leadership of the Argentine Labor Federation (*Central de los Trabajadores Argentinos*), various movements associated with the *Piqueteros* (unemployed people) federations, Mothers of the Plaza de Mayo, Jubilee South America and Movement for Peace, Sovereignty and Solidarity among Peoples (MOPASSOL[23]). This explains why in addition to trade, the topics of poverty, debt and militarization were included in the title of this movement.

Commonly known as the Self-Convoctory campaign, it organized two major national consultations in the form of popular referendums during 2003 and 2004. Mobilizing a wide range of social organizations and actors, the voting was held around the country asking people to express their opinion on the perceived consequences of the FTAA. The first consultation suggested that 96 percent of the Argentinean population considered the FTAA to be plainly negative to the country's general interest. This gave considerable legitimacy to the movement, as well as newly elected Kirchner's presidential team (Bidaseca and Rossi 2008: 73–74). The second consultation was organized around the effects of the FTAA, debt burdens and United States military bases on the life and social cohesion of the ordinary Argentinean people and natural resources. This consultation gathered less public enthusiasm, because the arrival of the Kirchner government and subsequent rapprochement of certain social movements (notably the Piqueteros) to the government set off to produce tensions and divisions within the Self-Convoctory campaign (ibid. 77).

Nevertheless, its unequivocal opposition to the FTAA continued to unite many of the social forces behind this organization. In addition to this, regional and continental social movements, especially labor federations, sought to pool resources together. As part of this action, the Self-Convoctory campaign was given the responsibility of organizing a Peoples Summit at the FTAA meeting held in Buenos Aires on January 1, 2005. The formal FTAA meeting was attended by numerous presidents, including the United States President George W. Bush. The Self-Convoctory together with the Continental Social Alliance (CSA) of trade unions organized workshops, public demonstrations, the media encounters and a major open air gathering in a stadium with a keynote speech by Hugo Chavez. With the participation of nearly 40,000 people, "the event was a political and media success" (ibid. 80–81). Although the Self-Convoctory lost dynamism within the country following the Peoples' Summit, given that trade issues began to acquire political and continental significance, its participation in regional activities and events have constantly been solicited by various trade union and social movement networks.

The movement against trade liberalization in Bolivia encompassed many similar facets to those just seen in Argentina. There was a widespread public perception that, first, globalization and opening of the national economy brought little or no benefits to the vast majority of the Bolivian people (Peeler 2004: 182–183). Second, the trade liberalization process merely helped to reinforce the prevailing United States' political and economic domination in the region. Third, the composition and objective of the movement against trade liberalization in Bolivia, including its regional and international alliance patterns, were very analogous to that of Argentina. But there were also certain differences, such as the proposition of Evo Morales to create a "Peoples Trade Treaty" involving Bolivia, Cuba and Venezuela. Another difference was the strong presence in the country of an Oxfam-led "trade justice movement" campaigning for improved access to the Northern markets for Southern products.

Following a formal decision to unleash a major continental campaign against FTAA at the WSF in Porto Alegre in February 2002, the Bolivian Movement of Fight against AFTA[24] and the FTAA (*Mouvimiento Boliviano de Lucha contre TLC et ALCA*) were created in May 2002. Bringing together a number of peasant and artisan organizations, NGOs and foundations, its initial discourses, meetings and publications stressed the need to disclose the various hidden clauses behind these two treaties, as well as their perceived negative impacts on the Bolivian economy and national sovereignty. Some of the actions proposed included information dissemination, close monitoring of national and international trade negotiations, elaboration of alternative proposals, holding of referendums to gauge peoples' views and development of campaigns on distinct problematic areas such as the national ownership and management of water and gas resources.

The ultimate purpose this campaign was obviously to prevent the government from negotiating and signing new trade accords. To propel these ideas and link the movement to local political dynamics, it organized several encounters of national, regional and international social organizations and networks in Cochabamba, including a Peoples Social Summit in December 2006. This summit brought together 4,000 activists, as well as the presidents of Bolivia, Venezuela and Nicaragua and the vice president of Argentina (Mayorga and Cordova 2008: 83).

As previously mentioned, significantly, the civil society campaign against trade treaties in the country received an unconditional backing from President Evo Morales. As a result, from the beginning of 2007, the Bolivian government policies began to reflect chiefly the civil society position. These policies included a forthright call to reject the negotiation of the United

States–led AFTA and FTAA treaties, on the one hand, and the initiation of a Peoples' Trade Treaty linking the neighboring socialist countries, on the other. As for the social movements, many of the key activists chose to join the government administration to provide advice and leadership on these various trade and social development matters.

International campaigners actively denounced the negative effects of trade negotiations for African economies ever since the GATT (General Agreement on Tariffs and Trade) was set up. The case of Senegal has been typical of a general African situation: the existence of a traditional agrarian economy with a great deal of dependency on the export of primary commodities. Yet in addition to a highly fluctuating price, the country continued to confront many types of trade barriers in rich countries (in the form of selection of certain products, customs duties, additional quality controls, etc.). At the same time, the signing of the latest trade rounds of treaties by Senegal meant an obligation for the country to open up its domestic market for foreign products. Here again the richer countries tended to largely benefit, owing to the ability to provide their producers with substantial production and export subsidies. At times, certain surplus food items were sold at prices frequently lower than those of local products. The ill-fate of the local and regional cotton and poultry industry as a result of the dumping of surplus cotton by the United States and chicken wings by the European Union has been widely cited; and research in recent years has shown similar trends for many crucial agricultural products, including rice, groundnuts, onions and potatoes (Dansokho 2007: 45–63).

As a result, trade issues constituted an important mobilizing factor among varieties of social organizations in the country, such as trade unions, consumers associations, producer cooperatives, NGOs, youth bodies, etc. The international NGOs like Oxfam and Christian Aid often served as the focal point. These organizations typically offered financial support to their counterpart organizations involved in trade justice campaigns. They also financed travel costs of the representatives of these organizations for participating in important regional and international meetings (Diop 2007: 12–23).

As for the national organizations, the consequences of trade liberalization in Senegal were taken up by wide-ranging social movements (although largely in a disparate fashion without any central organization body). The Enda tiers-monde, National Council of Rural Dialogue and Cooperation (CNCR[25]) and National Union of Senegalese Tradesmen and Industrialists (UNACOIS[26]) commonly raised trade issues in their work programs. However, since the arrival of Oxfam and Christian Aid in the early 2000s and their capacity to offer financial aid, organizations like the CONGAD, African Network for Integrated Development (RADI[27]), CNCR and Platform of African Students for Fair Trade (PEACE[28]) developed a number of concrete campaign programs on the consequences of trade liberalization corresponding largely to the global campaigns of these powerful international NGOs. Drawing on these and other sources of foreign funding, national organizations also initiated various awareness-raising activities on the broader consequences of trade talks. For this purpose, they published bulletins and newsletters and organized thematic meetings. In some cases, these organizations also offered training courses to producers so as to inform them on the quality, hygiene, production and preservation norms applied at the international level. They also endeavored to influence business people and government officials by explaining to them the content and potential effects of different international trade accords. Finally, they publicized the lack of transparency and weakness embedded in the government's trade negotiation procedures and outcomes.

With regard to the Philippines, the international campaign against trade liberalization was most favorably received, particularly for the following two reasons. First, there was a widespread concern that international trade accords negotiated by the government within the framework of the WTO could produce many detrimental effects to the country's agricultural sector. This stance was commonly shared by many transnational campaign networks as well. Second, several of the national NGOs were already an integral part of many of these international networks. This was notably the case with the FDC, as seen above. The choice of taking up Manila as an international headquarter by the Jubilee South was no doubt a clear testimony of these growing national and international fusions. In a similar manner, the Focus on the Global South, a potent Southeast Asian regional network on international trade and the broader consequences of globalization, decided to maintain its headquarters in Manila.

Linking directly with international groups, several national campaign organizations were created to promote debates on the consequences of trade liberalization in the country at different GATT negotiations, APEC and Asian summits. In 2003, the Stop the New Round Coalition (SNR) was established bringing together thirty-six social organizations. Indeed, the Focus on the Global South housed the secretariat of this organization. The principal activities of the SNR included the organizing of public rallies and demonstrations, media advocacy, engagement with the government and awareness-raising. It also sent a 15 member delegation to the Cancun WTO meeting in September 2003 in order to build international coalitions and to exert pressure onto the Philippine negotiators. At the international level, the SNR was linked to Our World Is Not For Sale (OWINFS), a global campaign that strongly opposed the Multilateral Agreement on Investment[29] (MAI) and the WTO accords. Working with the OWINFS, the SNR was able to build expedient relationships with several continental and regional movements from North America, Europe and Latin America. During this time, it also managed to obtain useful information on the ongoing negotiation processes, including certain classified data and documents on various sectors of the national economy under negotiation (Quinsaat 2009: 78).

While the SNR was able to make important gains through a close coalition with OWINFS, certain authors raised the question about its autonomy. Indeed, the SNR was "heavily influenced" by the OWINFS in its conception and activities. Furthermore, it failed to link up sufficiently with the Philippine government. Consequently, "the SNR was left out of trade negotiations during committee and general council meetings and became merely reactive on some points" (Tadem 2009c: 243).

In addition to OWINFS, the SNR received financial support from numerous international NGOs, notably the Canadian Catholic Church, Coalition of the Flemish North-South Movement in Belgium and Oxfam Great Britain and Oxfam Netherlands Novib. These two latter organizations were engaged in the *Make Trade Fair* campaign. However, this particular campaign, as well as the positions of the Western Churches on debt tended to be generally quite restrained. On the other hand, the OWINFS called for a sweeping transformation in the existing international systems of trading and economic relations. It also held a plainly antagonistic posture towards the international financial and commercial agencies and business groups. Given that the SNR derived its backing and resources from these two reformist and radical campaign networks, it was difficult to see where its intentions lay and what specific impact it was actually trying to make. In any event, the movement was already considerably weakened by the time the WTO negotiation took place in Hong Kong in 2005 (Quinsaat 2009: 92–93).

CURRENCY TRANSACTION TAX CAMPAIGN

The inspiration to impose a currency transaction tax was brought into Argentina by the Argentinean intellectuals previously associated with the French left. Against the background of a sharp decline in the Argentinean peso, capital flight, hyperinflation and the country's massive debt, the proposal to taxing or controlling the free circulation of speculative capital made a great deal of sense. Attac Argentina, started originally by a handful leftist economists, briskly attracted wide varieties of social, political and religious forces, including Peronists, Christian democrats and liberation theologists.[30] Interestingly, it was also Attac Argentine that laid down the conditions for the establishment of Attac branches in Chile, Bolivia and Uruguay (Rossi 2008: 239). It established two national committees, one in Buenos Aires and another one in Rosario. To generate heightened public interest, it organized several meetings, intervened in the media and, like in Europe, sought to mobilize the national parliament around the Tobin tax question. However, until 2001 its overall impact remained quite muted. As mentioned previously, the reason for this was simple: in the face of the gravity of the political and economic turbulence, Attac's proposal to regulate the market by merely seeking to impose a small currency transaction tax was considered by many social movements not to be sufficiently antagonistic so as to attract supporters (ibid. 247).

From 2002 onwards, the movement changed its strategy to adopt a more militant line of advocacy. In particular, the movement abandoned more or less the Tobin tax proposal to concentrate entirely on the campaign to the Self-Convoctory No to the FTAA. In actual fact, it hosted the headquarters of the campaign in its office and shared computers and other resources at hand. It played an energetic role in organizing the popular consultations held in 2003 and 2004, as well as the Peoples Summit at the FTAA gathering in Buenos Aires in 2005. In 2006 and 2007, Attac Argentina established a close association with the Kirchner administration, especially within the framework of a program titled "Encounter for Popular Sovereignty" (a government initiative to encourage debates on political alternatives emerging from a wide range of social forces). Its intellectual asset was recognized both within the government and civil society circles. Nevertheless, working with the government was a tricky business for a social movement considering the risk of cooptation, as well as the peril of further distancing itself from the grass roots.

Attac Bolivia emerged out of a curious affiliation of the French monthly anti-globalization journal *Le monde diplomatique* and a Bolivian citizen of a German-Polish Jewish origin: Günter Holzmann. With his anti-fascist background during World War II and his concern for a growing worldwide societal inequality and environmental damage prompted him to come into contact with the journal proposing to provide it with a core capital of up to 1 million USD[31] (Ramonet 2001). Since this journal and the Attac movement were intimately tied at the international level, the founding of the Attac Bolivia was a further step towards the consolidation of his growing intellectual and militant relationships with the international anti-globalization circle. In the meantime, Holzmann died. Thus, Attac Bolivia was formally established in May 2001 honoring the memory of this very personality in presence of the representatives from Attac France, Argentina, Brazil, Chile and Uruguay, in addition to the Bolivian social activists.

Three branches of the organization were opened, one in Santa Cruz, another one in La Paz and a third one in Cochabamba. By this time, the first edition of the 2001 WSF had already taken place in Porto Alegre and Attac national chapters were established in numerous countries. Attac Bolivia began mobilizing social organizations, citizens and formal institutional actors to rally towards the objective of making the dictum of "another world is possible"[32] a reality. It privileged electronic means of communication to send information and documents to a wide number of people and organizations. In the Santa Cruz area, parliamentarians were contacted. In La Paz, it held forums and "Attac Saturdays" (involving informal meetings in a café) and also published articles on the problematic of the autonomous national exploitation of gas resources. In Cochabamba, it sought to establish preliminary links and sporadic meetings with the activists associated with the anti-trade liberalization movement, although these efforts did not thrive much. Nor did its contacts prosper with parliamentarians and political parties. In the meantime, the new Evo Morales government started to concentrate its efforts on handling the burning issues of debt and trade negotiations. In short, Attac Bolivia did not succeed to go beyond the initial launching of a novel idea for a currency transaction tax in the public arena. Ultimately the entire initiative collapsed, as described Mayorga and Cordova:

> Gradually, the contacts were lost and the web sites of Attac Bolivia ceased to function; nevertheless, some members of the committee were present in the Porto Alegre forum, although, without relations with the representatives of the current Bolivian social movements, which, in some cases, were the protagonists in the debates. (Mayorga and Cordova 2008: 172)

Attac Senegal was established in 1998, in other words, the same year as the founding of Attac France. For obvious historical reasons, an organic relationship has tended to exist between intellectuals and social movements in both countries.[33] Many of the intellectuals would have often graduated from the same universities in France and thus facilitating them to form part of the numerous joint networks in the field of academia, journalism or social activism. The majority of these intellectuals also came from the left-wing tradition. As such, the central premise of the movement that taxation on speculative capital would create additional resources for social welfare and economic development and that it would give the State more power over financial management and control appeared apposite and acquiescent for these intellectuals in both countries.

The prime mode of working of the Senegalese chapter of Attac, right from its launch, was to organize public meetings and debates involving a wide range of actors, such as the academics, trade unionists, students, parliamentarians and specialists from the development projects. A common inference of these gatherings was that capital movements needed to be regulated so as to stabilize and build up the national economy. At the same time, it was thought that the Senegalese or African situation required major adaptation in the movement's scope and operational objectives.

Subsequently, Attac Senegal spearheaded, in addition to the issue of the Tobin tax campaign, combining the critical questions of debt reduction, a stable price for raw materials, corruption control, putting an end to privatization, environmental protection and an enhanced protection of civil liberties and democracy.[34] The diffusion of vital information and documents though the Internet was actively carried out, although during the time of the writing of this text (in January 2010) the organization's Internet site appeared already considerably unfurnished and inoperative.

Nevertheless, the issue of Tobin tax was discussed by some parliamentarians, and in August 2005 the Senegalese National Assembly authorized to install an air ticket tax to finance the construction and maintenance of the country's airport infrastructure (Daffe 2007: 80–93). During this time, at the initiative of the French president Chirac, an enthusiastic debate was taking place at the international level regarding the prospects of imposing an air ticket levy to finance development activities in poor countries. It is difficult to observe if there had been any direct effects of the mobilization capacity of Attac Senegalese on these various evolutions at the national level. Perceptibly, the organization did help to sustain the debate justifying the usefulness of the currency transaction tax to generating additional resources for vital development interventions. For the same reason, it continued to argue that the general economic improvements were viable only through important debt relief measures, stable export prices and the recovery in public services.

Debates on the international currency taxation mounted by Attac and other associated organizations in Europe and North America had certain reverberations in the Philippines, too, in large part because this coincided with the 1997 Asian financial crisis. In early 1999, the Third World Network (TWN), a regional anti-globalization think tank based in Penang, Malaysia, circulated a call in the region for seeking to mobilize social forces to push for a levy on currency transactions so as to deter speculative activities on capital transactions. The response from the academics, parliamentarians and civil society organizations in the Philippines was fairly passive (Molmisa 2009: 113). Among the academics, the principal group interested in exploring this field was the economists closely connected to the new democratic Aquino government. Yet they were very careful not to propose too sweeping measures going totally against the conciliatory economic policies pursued by the new administration. Certain parliamentarians with influence coming from European parliamentarians sought to examine the topic, but these initiatives remained generally limited to sponsoring a parliamentarian study, as was mentioned earlier. Typically, it was within the NGOs and social movements circle that the issue of currency transaction was considered more earnestly.

With varying degrees, four social organizations promoted the discussion on the idea and benefits of currency transaction taxation in the country.

The first was the Alliance of Progressive Labor (a nationwide coalition of trade unions). It sought to examine the relationships between financial instabilities and their negative effects on job creations and the usefulness of the Tobin tax to stabilize financial markets. In line with the call from its union affiliations at the international level, it argued that collective bargaining was no longer sufficient in the absence of essential fiscal and monetary controls (ibid. 124).

Likewise, the FDC (the second group to work in this area) argued that debt and financial instabilities were intimately linked since the financial volatility and capital flows tended to directly affect the country's ability to repay its foreign debt. Enjoying a prominent international reputation, this organization was commonly invited to take part in regional and international meetings in this area, including a conference organized by the Attac international movement in Cologne in March 1999.

During this time, the Focus on the Global South (a third important organization) also became active in campaigning for the need to establish effective mechanisms for capital controls. However, the organization rapidly "shelved" Tobin tax advocacy in favor of international trade and related issues (ibid. 123–124).

Finally, the Action for Economic Reforms (AER), an independent research and policy analysis organization, undertook a study and published several papers describing how speculative portfolio investments could be controlled, in part through the merit of the Tobin tax measures. In collaboration with the Asian Regional Exchange for New Alternatives (ARENA), it organized an international meeting in Hong Kong in February 2001. This meeting suggested that strong capital control measures would have saved the region from a disastrous financial crisis in 1997 (AER 2001).

It is clear that much of this debate was limited to a relatively short period (1999–2001), thus immediately following the Asian financial crisis. International campaigns such as Attac France and its other Northern branches gave heightened attention to the region. After this period, most of the national organizations initially displaying the interest in the idea of a currency transaction taxation steadily moved away to other areas. Despite a general agreement among most social actors in the country on the need to regulate capital markets as well as the prospects for creating supplementary financial resources for social welfare through the currency transaction initiatives, the Attac campaign demonstrated only a limited national significance in the Philippines.

Anti-Corruption Campaign

In the 1980s, with a keen interest in promoting democratic consolidation and financial accountability, international donor agencies sought to support Argentinean NGOs and human rights organizations. Some of these latter forces reoriented themselves to work closely in the area of corruption. In some ways the international agenda and a growing national concern for corruption met rather auspiciously. Corruption was a critical issue of disquiet already in the early 1980s, and this has been so throughout the past 25 years irrespective of the nature of the political regimes or socio-economic crises. Gradually, corruption was recognized as a serious problem by political parties (from both the left and the right), religious groups and the business community. The denunciation of a generalized corruption was also a recurrent subject matter in popular mobilizations at the local level (Nardacchione 2006: 43 and 94; Auyero 2005: 250–268).

The key Argentinean anti-corruption organization, the Citizen Power (*Poder Ciudadanio*), was established in 1989, hence several years prior to the founding of the Transparency International in 1993. In the early years of its work, the organization was concerned with the protection of broader civil rights. In the mid to late1990s, its work focused more closely on the question of "social accountability" issues involving the over-concentration of power in the hands of the executive (i.e., the president) and the lack of a judicial autonomy. A general argument advanced was that the political delegation could "no longer be based on a basic trust in the personal qualities of those in power" but needed to be "transferred to a set of impersonal safeguards that protect the citizenry against eventual breaches of trust by authorities" (Peruzzotti 2005: 233). In concrete terms, this meant monitoring the functioning of public officials and agencies, exposing the cases of unlawful activities and undertaking independent investigation on the impartiality in the provisioning of public services (ibid. 236). Besides, this meant putting accent on raising public awareness, disseminating useful information and carrying out data collection and thematic research. For achieving this goal, the organization used journalists, lawyers and academic people; and it also sought to maintain a good working relationship with the business sector and the government (Pereyra 2008: 107–110).

The Citizen Power was never a formal branch of the TI. Nonetheless, it maintained fairly a close relationship. For example, it provided the TI with national data on corruption perceptions, and functioned as a close affiliate for TI's international meetings and corruption control projects in the region. For many international development agencies, the Citizen Power was a model civil society organization to fund and collaborate. As such, international NGOs, campaigns and academic groups seeking to work in the field of corruption in the country could not afford to circumvent it. On the whole, the organization remained fairly conformist in its approach. Much of its funds came from the agencies like the USAID and National Endowment for Democracy (a US group working on human rights linked to the Republican Party), Ford Foundation and United Nations Development Program (UNDP). It also kept distance from Third World radicals at the international level as they tended to generally argue that many of the anti-corruption measures proposed in recent years represented basically the Northern donor agencies' perception and a ploy to impose further economic and political conditionality on the South. Similarly, nationally, it avoided taking an active part in militant politics, local assemblies, forums or popular demonstrations. One reason for this was that Citizen Power always sought to keep itself away from the partisan party politics. On the other hand, this made the organization remain outside many of the emerging social mobilization processes in the country such as the World Social Forum or campaigns against the FTAA.

As for Bolivia, an organized national campaign on corruption control has emerged only very recently. This is so despite the fact that corruption has remained a widespread occurrence within politics, the bureaucracy and the judiciary system. Indeed, the term "politician" itself has a very negative connotation in public perception, basically suggesting a shady person with good words but greatly profiting from the country's economic crisis and deprivation (Suarez 2005: 146). As an international image building effort, a top governmental anti-corruption body, named the Presidential Anticorruption Delegation (DPA[35]) was established in 2003 by President Carlos Mesa. Its principal objective was to uncover, prevent and investigate corruption cases, as well as sanction those found responsible. The DPA also regarded the participation of civil society organizations in corruption control activities as being very important. The creation of the Territorial Citizens Network against Corruption (*Las Redes Ciudadanas Anticorrupción Territoriales*) was the direct result of this initiative.

The principal non-governmental organization specialized in the field of corruption, the Citizens' Anticorruption Move (*La Movida Ciudadana Anticorrupción*), was established in 2003 with financial support from the DPA. It expanded its scope considerably after many of the former staff of the DPA joined it, bringing in new resources and skills. It developed intervention activities to promote honesty and open public access to information.

Another organization, established in 2001 within the framework of the Inter American Convention against Corruption, was the Ethics and Democracy Foundation (*la Fundación Ética y Democracia*). As its name suggests, its main line of reasoning was that the ethical standard needed to be elevated in every walk of public life. This agency acted as the leading national contact institution for the TI.

There was also the presence of the Carter Foundation; Franciscans launched an anti-corruption campaign called "Honest Day"; and the Pueblo Foundation unveiled a program aimed at empowering popular participation in corruption control. A number of university centers also commonly conducted research on corruption issues. Finally, in more recent years, several Internet projects have emerged with the mandate of uncovering and disseminating information on the most flagrant cases of corruption (Mayorga and Cordova 2008: 151–154). Unfailingly, all these initiatives have been financed by external sources.

Evo Morales expressed support to corruption control measures soon after being elected as the country's president, namely by establishing in April 2006 a National Council for Fight against Corruption (*Consejo Nacional de Lucha contre la Corruption*). A principal line of argument was that transparency in public institutions was urgently needed to impede the wider prevailing mechanisms of social discrimination and exclusion. This conception, no doubt fundamentally exact, had the weakness of leaving out the practical side of corruption in the past. This was particularly the case with the actions undertaken by most of the traditional social movements (peasant and labor unions, left-wing parties, etc.) in this area (ibid. 8). In other words, these social forces tended to limit themselves to a general discourse against the fraudulent and unjust political and economic structures without proposing or seeking to implement any concrete corruption control projects in specific contexts.

In Senegal, the Civil Forum (FC[36]) was the leading organization involved in the anti-corruption campaign. Established in 1993, it worked on a low scale until it was chosen by the TI in 2000 to formally become its national branch. Under this organizational link, the FC began to disseminate the information produced by the TI, as well as integrate TI's various approaches and methods in its work programs. In return, as we'll see later, it received important international political endorsement and protection. This collaboration also helped to legitimize the FC's leading role in corruption campaign among civil society organizations in the country. In fact, following its major international recognition, it began to invite several social organizations working in the area of human rights, women and youth, on religious matters, and trade unions and employers' organizations to form a broad anti-corruption coalition directly under its leadership.

The work of the FC gradually changed both in scope and scale. In the 1990s, the organization was involved in politically less sensitive issues like the investigation of financial frauds in environmental or heath projects and question of women's representation to political institutions such as the local municipalities. After having gained its new international stature and especially the improved accessibility to international funding as a result, it moved towards developing a more forthright program on the "transparency" in the attribution of tenders for public works and fair conduct of elections. It also launched training programs on investigative journalism and civil servant integrity in customs, tax office and local municipalities. It coordinated data collection and research activities. Likewise, with the availability of external funding, it spearheaded an active mass communication project, including the attempt to establish direct links with the press and develop an interactive Internet website.

In spite of this, the FC confronted severe difficulties, namely on the following two fronts. First, in Senegal, like in many developing countries, there has been a persistent incidence of patrimonial behaviors and personalization of power. For example, President Wade, who had pledged a full and transparent democracy while in opposition, once elected in 2000, "blurred the distinction between public and private resources by distributing monthly supplements to the salaries of governors and other officials in the territorial administration and giving leaders of political parties in his coalition monthly stipends" (Gellar 2005: 157). Despite the fact that, the principles of good governance and transparent management were included in the national constitution, the government was not willing to accept the findings of the FC's work until pressure from the TI and funding agencies (Thioub 2007: 37–40). Even so corruption continued to affect all levels of public administration, often with the complaisance of political elites and the judiciary system. Second, the FC faced difficulties in mobilizing the public opinion around corruption. For example, an opinion poll in December 2006, carried out by the Afrobarometer group in collaboration with the FC, suggested that corruption was only the 16th priority area, with employment, food, health, agriculture and livestock receiving the prime attention.[37]

Finally, concerning the experience of the anti-corruption advocacy in the Philippines, the Transparency and Accountability Network (TAN), established during the anti-corruption mobilizations against President Joseph Estrada in 2000, functioned as the largest anti-corruption social organization. It was a coalition of NGOs, social movements, research centers, the representatives from the business community and funding agencies. The TI Philippines was a member of this endeavour. The general objectives of the TAN included: the raising of public awareness on the economic and political effects of corruption, mobilizing of the general public through the use of collective votes and actions and raising of corruption as a key issue for policy intervention. As such, it sought to work closely with the government.

Wui suggests that, unlike debt, trade and currency taxation movements "whose inspiration was derived at the international level, TAN is an initiative that came about because of the efforts and occurrences at the local level" (Wui 2009: 208–209). At the same time, in its approach, functioning and resource mobilization, the movement was heavily influenced by dominant conceptions and the availability of external financial resources. For example, it functioned largely within the framework developed by international bodies in that corruption was considered a fundamental prerequisite to achieving good governance at the national level. The World Bank, USAID and UNDP were consistently the chief financiers of the TAN.

The preceding illustrations may suffice to suggest that transnational movements on debt relief, trade justice, currency transactions taxation and anti-corruption injected certain dynamism in mobilization capacity at the national level. In some cases, the themes themselves were imported from outside. We can safely say that this was very much the case with debt advocacy since campaign ideas, finance and international and regional networking prospects were possible in large part thanks to an active preparation of the Jubilee 2000 by Church groups and international NGOs. The debates on the currency transaction taxation also came from abroad, introduced for the most part by the Attac movement. As for the campaign against trade liberalization, the international influence remained all but extremely important in developing major national and regional protests. Finally, the international anti-corruption campaign, based around the consolidation of democracy and sound management of the business and economic practices and pushed by international donor agencies, the US foundations, the TI and numerous other international agencies and NGOs, was the prime instigator behind nearly all major anti-corruption mobilizations at the national level. Overall the dimensions of debt, trade, financial transactions tax and anti-corruption were not absent in the public debate at the national level, as was seen in the previous section. However, the framing of issues politically and mounting of longer-term activities were the direct result of the connectivity with the transnational campaigns.

Having said this, organizational linkages between international and national groups were based on informal and occasional collaborations. Furthermore, despite sharing of general values, such collaborations were not directed to any organized or sustained collective actions. Internet communications, interactions with delegates at international gatherings and most crucially the contacts with selected influential individuals (based on ideological/intellectual and language affinities) were the most common mechanisms that helped them to frequently link up. This has no doubt been a fairly familiar feature within much of the alternative globalization movement. Nevertheless, despite this sporadic nature of cooperation, the national groups were not in a position to join or abandon the international network at their will. This instead steadily put them in a dependent relationship vis à vis international groups. Thus, referring again to the work of Tarrow and McAdam on the scale shift in transnational contention, we can see that, despite the attempt to identify a common cause or engaging in similar action, there is no guarantee that national and international movements hold exactly the same degree of resources or possibility to exert influence. It is precisely this latter feature that we propose to examine more closely in the following chapter.

NOTES

1. BBC (British Broadcasting Corporation). http://www.news.bbc.com.uk/2/hi/business/4533740.stm (accessed May 5, 2010).

2. World Bank. http://www.data.worldbank.org/indicator/DT.DOD.DECT.CD (accessed May 5, 2010).

3. Transparency International. http://www.transparency.org.policy_research/surveys_indices/ (accessed May 5, 2010).

4. World Bank. http://www.data.worldbank.org/indicator/NE.EXP.GNFS.ZS (accessed May 5, 2010).

5. World Bank. http://www.data.worldbank.org/indicator/SI.DST.FRST.20 (accessed May 5, 2010).

6. World Bank. http://www.data.worldbank.org/indicator/DT.DOD.DECT.CD (accessed May 5, 2010).

7. Transparency International. http://www.transparency.org.policy_research/surveys_indices/ (accessed May 5, 2010).

8. World Bank. http://www.data.worldbank.org/indicator/NY/GDP.MKTP.KD.ZG (accessed May 5, 2010).

9. A study by the National Institute of Statistics indicated that in 2006 the export of Bolivian products to the US created only about 23,000 jobs, with an annual income of 40 million USD (National Institute of Statistics. http://www.udape.gov.bo/notas%20de%20coyuntura/Notas3.pdf (accessed February 14, 2010).

10. World Bank. http://www.data.worldbank.org/indicator/SI.DST.FRST.20 (accessed May 5, 2010).

11. World Bank. http://fr.allafrica.com/stories/200802060859.html (accessed May 5, 2010).

12. World Bank. http://www.data.worldbank.org/indicator/DT.DOD.DECT.CD (accessed May 5, 2010).

13. World Bank. http://www.data.worldbank.org/indicator/NE.EXP.GNFS.ZS (accessed May 5, 2010).

14. Transparency International. http://www.transparency.org.policy_research/surveys_indices/ (accessed May 5, 2010).

15. World Bank. http://www.data.worldbank.org/indicator/DT.DOD.DECT.CD (accessed May 5, 2010).

16. Transparency International. http://www.transparency.org.policy_research/surveys_indices/ (accessed May 5, 2010).

17. An association of Argentine mothers whose children "disappeared" during the military dictatorship between 1976 and 1983.

18. *Comité pour l'annulation de la dette du tiers monde.*

19. *Conseil des ONG d'appui au développement.*

20. *Réseau des plateformes nationales d'ONG d'Afrique de l'Ouest et du Centre.*

21. *Union nationale des sydicats autonomes du Sénégal.*

22. *Forum social sénégalais.*

23. *Movimiento por la Paz, la Soberanía y la Solidaridad de los Pueblos.*

24. The trade treaty between the US and Andean nations: Andean Free Trade Agreement (AFTA).

25. *Conseil national de concertation et de coopération des ruraux.*

26. *Union nationale des commençants et industriels du Sénégal.*

27. *Réseau africain pour le développement intégré.*

28. *La Plateforme des étudiants africains pour le commerce équitable.*

29. A draft agreement negotiated between the members of the OECD in the late 1990s seeking to foster unhindered foreign investment (see OECD, 1998, http://www1.oecd.org/daf/mai/pdf/ng/ng987r1e.pdf). Civil society campaigners were concerned that market forces were given an uncontrolled supremacy over the State's capacity to regulate the economy. With pressure from social organizations and common citizens in the country, in 1998, the French socialist government withdrew from the agreement, thereby ultimately killing the treaty.

30. Liberation theologists mixed Marxism with Christian teachings. The notion of "liberation theology" emerged in Latin America in the 1960s and 1970s as a moral crusade against the unjust economic, political and social conditions faced by the masses, especially the peasantry. There was a strong emphasis on conscious-raising through literacy campaigns (see, for example, Freire 1970).

31. Facing major financial difficulties, during this time the journal had called upon its "friends" to participate in raising vital operating funds.

32. Details on this conception are included in part 3.

33. It should also be noted that in recent years the Senegalese intellectuals have attempted to increasingly internationalize themselves by developing links with the English-speaking world.

34. Attac Senegal. http://www.attac.org/senegal/calandrier.html (accessed January 11, 2010).

35. *La Delegación Presidencial Anticorrupción.*

36. *Forum civil.*

37. Afrobarometer. http://www.forumcivil.sn/spip.php?article36# (accessed January 12, 2009).

3

International Influence and Dependence

The transnational campaigns on debt relief, trade justice, currency taxation and anti-corruption stemmed from multiple social bases. They maintained a varying degree of relationships with the public institutions. Furthermore, they diverged somewhat in the level of overall radicalism that was considered necessary in bringing about desired societal changes. Nonetheless, all four campaigns remained very much identical in their pursuit to popularize their central message. Indeed, reaching out to wider territories and population groups was nearly obligatory owing to their need to have to speak out for poorer countries in the Southern hemisphere. This was also essential for the purpose of enlisting new supporters and recruits who could potentially be mobilized, particularly in mounting activities at global events such as the international conferences.

Concurrently, as observed above, the principal national organizations working in these areas held philosophical and strategic approaches very similar to their respective international counterparts. In most cases, they displayed a great deal of willingness to craft activities in response to the demands formulated at the international level. In short, there existed considerable prospects for collaboration, if not complete complicity, between transnational movements and the key organizations active at the national level. Despite this, their priorities and interests were not exactly the same. Most of all, the national level actors stood out to be fairly unequal in their ability to hold crucial resources and have an overall organizational influence.

DEBT RELIEF MOVEMENT

Grimson and Pereyra argue in the case of Argentina that national arenas "will not be mechanically replaced by supranational structures on a new *mapa mundi* any time soon" (Grimson and Pereyra 2008b: 19). This seemed certainly to be true with respect to the anti-debt movement as a whole and Dialogue 2000 in particular. However, a significant international stimulus occurred influencing directly the national debates on the debt question. Dialogue 2000 eagerly greeted international influence since first and foremost its prime objectives strongly corresponded to the international advocacy agenda. Furthermore, transnational campaigns injected fresh ideas and financial resources. The organization's principal assertion that the country's vast debt produced huge and pervasive social costs in terms of human rights violations and economic wellbeing of the common people was something fairly agreeable to most international actors. It also pleaded for greater solidarity among people, the principles of non-violence, and protection of fundamental individual rights (Rivkin 2008: 164). These sorts of inspirations were commonly being discussed within the international church movement and Third World activist groups globally, principally in the process of preparing for the Jubilee 2000 event. These evolutions helped Dialogue 2000 most positively to establish increased international contacts and most crucially obtain essential funds. The international connection also represented a new space for the organization in its attempt to widely publicize the country's debt dilemmas.

At the same time, given the seriousness of the debt problem, in particular, and economic disaster, in general, and its "soft approach" to dealing with the debt crisis in line with the Jubilee 2000's more conciliatory demands for debt forgiveness at the international level, the organization remained largely imperceptible in the national public arena during the first few years of its inception. In specific, it maintained little or no contact with popular movements, opposition political parties, syndicates and other professional associations in the country.

The influence of the Jubilee South was a determinant factor for the organization to change this course. In line with the position of the Jubilee South, the organization commenced to argue that the country's debt contracted by the military junta in the past was entirely illegitimate. Accordingly, there was no justification for repaying it to the Western creditors and international financial institutions. The organization swiftly came into regional limelight. Nationally, as we have seen earlier, two important referendums were organized to mobilize public opinion against the FTAA. Dialogue 2000 succeeded in including the debt as one of the four key concerns to be jointly pushed by social movements (the other three issues being trade liberalization, militarization and poverty). Also, during this time, the organization was asked to host the Jubilee South Latin America headquarters. Furthermore, it sought to insert itself into the regional mobilization processes (namely to the holding of the World Social Forum in 2002 and Peoples Summit in 2005). In any event, many of these outcomes reflected the development of a defiant public opinion in the country, leading to the eventual unilateral default and significant renegotiation on foreign debt payment by the new Kirchner government.

A foremost strain experienced by Dialogue 2000 in more recent years has clearly been associated with the difficulties in securing financial resources for its program activities. Its funds came essentially from the church organizations in North America and Europe. Yet these organizations for the most part followed rather a moderate and charity-oriented approach in dealing with the debt and poverty issues in developing countries. In the meantime, Dialogue 2000 created a firm coalition with an exceptionally radical debt movement: the Jubilee South. This alliance attested politically expedient until 2005, when it began to show signs of complications in keeping up the momentum in its mobilization efforts given a visibly uncompromising approach of the Jubilee South. Besides, the Kirchner government began to occupy some of the same public space previously held by social movements, including the debt campaign.

With reference to Bolivia, too, despite the fact that foreign debt had become an extremely heavy burden for the country, the framing of the issue and many of the mobilization efforts were possible mainly through international affiliations and support. We saw already how the international discussion surrounding the HIPC debt relief measures created room for social mobilization, both at home and abroad. A principal element of this mobilization was the assertion that (owing to the human suffering and lower level of economic development) Bolivia merited full inclusion in the list of poor countries benefiting debt pardoning. This mobilization occurred in tandem with the preparation of the Jubilee 2000 event. In more recent years, the movement has been concerned with the question of transparency in the work of political parties and an optimum use of the available financial resources (including those coming through the HIPC debt relief measures) for various poverty reduction activities. On the other hand, most regional trade union federations, the World Social Forum and particularly the Jubilee South have continued to argue for the complete and unconditional annulations of the country's foreign debt as a prerequisite for any significant improvements in economic and social welfare conditions to occur.

While this gave rise to a substantial tension in the approach dealing with the debt problem, both the pragmatic and radical groups continued to attain external resources in the form of funds, contacts with global networks, and to a limited extent, the media. Without any doubt, in terms of accessing international financial resources, the first group enjoyed considerable

advantage, but the ensuing political events in the country steadily strength-
ened the position of the second. In any event, despite the forgiveness of
sizeable sums of debt, it became clear that the total amount of foreign debt
would continue to mount in the face of new loans and credits, thus reinforcing the demand for far-reaching economic and social reforms. Indeed,
according to certain observers, the arrival of the Morales government with
a radical agenda proposing to renegotiate the existing contracts with the
hydrocarbon sector in order to increase the pool of national income and
capacity to repay the country's outstanding debt have already begun to produce certain positive effects. Mayorga and Cordova elaborate this process
in the following terms:

> These renegotiations have already increased the percentage of taxes paid by
> those enterprises to the State between 18 to 82 percent. Moreover, the price
> of gas sold to Argentina and Brazil has been augmented. With a growing
> State's role in the economy, the foreign debt relief measures may have greater
> (positive) impact. In fact, this new policy on hydrocarbons allowed the State
> to finish 2006, after many years, without fiscal deficits. (Mayorga and Cordova
> 2008: 92)

As for Senegal, unlike Argentina or Bolivia, there existed no organized
debt cancellation campaign. The movement, albeit periodically animated
by various civil society organizations, remained quite imperceptible and
fragmented. Most of the activities mounted were directly in response to
international debates and proceedings. These included the various discussions surrounding the launching or exact size of the HIPC scheme to be
implemented, meetings of the G7 and international financial institutions,
and global civil society events such as the holding of the WSF. The existence
of a relatively good conference facility, international air-travel connections
and a generally stable political system with a vigorous associative tradition
was that Senegal stood to be an ideal African location for organizing intercontinental and regional meetings. This thus helped to create a significant
scope for the engagement of national organizations with international
campaigns and networks.

The Senegalese civil society organizations, on their part, were able to provide the transnational campaigns with input in their global mobilization
efforts, as well as run certain activities for them in the country or region.
At the same time, this also produced the effect of national organizations
having to modify their work primarily geared towards the organization of
the specific events or fulfillment of distinct tasks imposed upon them from
the international level. A usual result of this situation was that the national
mobilization against debt remained highly intermittent. Nevertheless, the
Senegalese NGOs and social movements attempted to chip in quite successfully in the initiatives created by transnational campaigns, emanating from
both the Francophone and Anglophone developed countries. In particular,

they succeeded in obtaining funds to launch certain program activities linked directly or indirectly to these international initiatives.

In a similar manner, in the Philippines, transnational connectivity was a decisive factor for the establishment of the FDC. The movement saw a rapid expansion in its work capacity and influence when the Western governments and international financial institutions began to consider financing the HIPC initiatives; and this happened parallel to the inception of the Jubilee 2000. The FDC's mobilization capacity and experience in dealing with the debt contracted under an autocratic regime was widely commended. Notably, the Jubilee movement (both the Jubilee 2000 and the Jubilee South) took on board its initial principal contention that the debt incurred during dictatorial and corrupt regimes was mostly dishonest and should therefore be repudiated. In the same manner, several of its leading activists and employees (former and present alike) were sought after as advisors or staff by various international bodies, including major NGOs and social movements working in the area of debt campaign.

One major direct benefit of this international standing was that the FDC gained an easy access to funds from external sources. Between 2000 and 2008, for example, it received more than 60 million PHP (nearly 15 million USD at the exchange rate of January 2008). This allowed the organization to be financially very much at ease. Indeed, as Ariate and Molmisa write:

> The activist group, besides funding research and protest actions, makes sure it has enough leftover money for a provident fund and a multipurpose fund, the first to finance separation pay and accident and medical benefits, and the second, to provide a forced savings scheme for the FDC officers and employees, with FDC matching the staff contributions. According to FDC records, it even has money to finance personal computer loans for its officers and rank and file. (Ariate and Molmisa, 2009: 41)

Without any doubt, many social organizations around the world would be envious of the kind of financial security that the FDC enjoyed. However, the arrival of important amounts of money was also the principal cause of its reduced visibility in debt activism and expansion of its program activities to all sorts of other areas, as we saw above. Increasingly, its core collaborators were international funding agencies and development NGOs, not political parties, syndicate groups, or academic centers, as it used to be typically the case in the past.

CAMPAIGN AGAINST TRADE LIBERALIZATION

The anti-trade liberalization campaign in Argentina held a significant regional and international connection. This link was possible in large part because of a shared anxiety among trade union organizations of the

negative consequences of regional trade agreements. The trade union organizations from North America were concerned that trade liberalization
could potentially produce detrimental employment effects in their countries (i.e., through the dislocation of industries to countries where labor
costs remained cheap and social and environmental legislative norms
weak, as well as the influx of cheap products from poorer countries).
This explained precisely why the North American trade union federations
were so actively engaged in organizing protest demonstrations against
trade liberalization talks in Seattle in 1999. The Argentinean trade unions
and other social movements, on the other hand, were nervous about the
ever-increasing sway of the United States' economic, political and military
strength in the country. Despite these varied interests, trade unions from
both North and South America could identify the trade liberalization treaties to be a common foe. This united position was keenly articulated in the
establishment of a joint CSA and the mounting of unified protests at trade
negotiation meetings from Miami in 1994 to Quebec in 2001 (Svampa
2005: 122–123).

So it seemed all but natural that continental trade federations would
also organize a major protest campaign at the FTAA Buenos Aires meeting
in 2005. By then, the Argentinean labor networks had become an integral
part of the CSA's campaign. Other notable regional or international social
organization networks that held a similar stance on the FTAA as well as the
US political and economic dominance in the region included the Jubilee
South and the WSF. In addition to this, a certain number of Latin American governments, notably Brazilian, Argentinean and Venezuelan, showed
a strong skepticism to the perceived benefits of the intercontinental trade
liberalization agreements. A successful organization of the Peoples Summit
at the 2005 FTAA Buenos Aires meeting was no doubt a combined outcome
of the fusion of these various ingredients.

Yet these regional and international connections were marked by tempo-
rality, since much of the activity undertaken was basically geared towards
the organization of single events. Consequently, The Self-Convoked No to
the FTAA proved a short-term initiative as it could not maintain dynamism
in its mobilization capacity during the post-event period. The national
leadership within the campaign against trade liberalization, too, began to
weaken slowly, with decision-making roles being concentrated again on
the regional and international networks. Another problematic area in this
regard was that, with trade negotiation issues fully on regional protests
agenda, mobilization activities moved from one country to another as if a
particular national setting mattered little. As for the financial dependency,
while around the time of the FTAA 2005 meeting, the Kirchner administration (as well as the Venezuelan government) funded a certain number of
activities, the North American trade union federations and the church or-

ganizations from the developed world continued to represent the primary sources of essential funds.

In Bolivia, the debates on the international trade liberalization went through three principal phases. During the first phase, much of the public debate was concerned with the issues of asymmetrical trade relationships between the poor and rich countries involving the GATT negotiations. Organizations such as Oxfam pushed the idea of "trade with justice" in support of small farming export-oriented agriculture in poor countries. There was a strong echo of this campaign in Bolivia, with Oxfam maintaining a sizeable program operation in the country.

The second phase began with the launching of the Bolivian Movement of Fight against AFTA and FTAA in 2002, coinciding with the major political upheavals unleashed by the Cochabamba water war. It is not out of the blue that two of the important international encounters which, among others, propelled the idea of a complete rejection of AFTA and FTAA were held in Cochabamba in 2002 and 2006. While the CSA, the WSF, Our World Is Not For Sale and Jubilee South continued to impel a general dynamism in the popular opposition to these trade treaties, these two international encounters organized in Cochabamba attracted many international networks of activists, media people, academics and documentary producers, as well as celebrities and left-wing State leaders from the region. This no doubt helped to gain valuable external contacts and a certain quantity of financial resources for national action.

Third phase comprised the election of Evo Morales as the country's president, with a clear shift "from the protest to the proposal." In any event, with the new government deciding not to enter into negotiations on either of the treaties and the intent to implement the FTAA being thoroughly paralyzed, there were no ardent justifications to continue to mount mobilization against the continental trade treaties. This caused the campaign to lose its original force, even if regionally it continued to operate, facilitating access to useful information and organizing meetings. Taking this development into account, the national chapter opted for a new name: Movement for Sovereignty and Solidarity Integrations of Peoples: Against AFTA and FTAA. It also decided to support the government's proposal to expand the concept of "Peoples Trade Treaty" aimed at reinforcing trade with neighboring socialist countries. While the overall impact of this new form of trade relations was still to be proven, there was already the risk of the key activists being absorbed by the government bureaucracy. Furthermore, given that the North-South trade relations constituted the core campaign issues for the continental trade federations and other transnational trade justice networks, there was no particular regional or international support readily forthcoming to the national groups seeking to work in this area.

With regard to the case of Senegal, although trade liberalization had steadily become an important concern among certain civil society organizations, it was usually the international NGOs like Oxfam and Christian Aid that actually galvanized the national movement. And this was so despite the fact that Oxfam's *Make Trade Fair* campaign asserting that just trade could be a source of shared prosperity and poverty reduction in the South was considered to be an insufficient proposition by many national movements given the existing political and economic world order (Diop 2007: 7–9). Oxfam landed in Senegal in 2002 on a big scale, as Diop writes:

> In Senegal the Oxfam family launched its campaign in 2002 at the Dakar Chamber of Commerce with attendance of several civil society partners intervening in Senegal and many invited guests from other sectors of international cooperation and the media. They shared their visions and experiences in matters of fair trade." (ibid. 14)

This citation is revealing the way international campaigns related to a national setting. First, Oxfam resurged at once in 2002; second, it organized its launching meeting at the national Chamber of Commerce (thus at a very officious location and in particular not at a social or public forum); third, the attending civil organizations were Oxfam's own "partners"; fourth, the invited people included mainly the representatives of the foreign aid sector and the media; and finally, the participants shared their visions and experiences with reference to what Oxfam basically presented at the meeting. So far as the engagement with the national civil society organizations were concerned, Oxfam decided to finance a certain number of projects relating to the translation of its campaign material into French, commissioning of punctual studies, organization of meetings, and covering of basic travel costs for some its collaborators to attend regional and international meetings.

Christian Aid, too, financed similar sorts of activities, including the preparation of a national report on trade campaign and participation of the Senegalese team in a Fair Trade World Campaign, held in New Delhi in 2005 (ibid. 17). A positive outcome of the involvement of international NGOs was the ability of national groups to internationalize the difficulties faced by Senegalese farmers and artisans following trade liberalization, especially those involved in cotton and poultry farming.

Predictably, there was little national ownership of the trade movement in Senegal. Many of the activities undertaken remained largely sporadic. Moreover, much of this had to be adjusted to external funding cycles. On the whole, the overwhelming role of the international campaigners such as Oxfam and Christian Aid, their specific methods of conceptualizing the issues and designing of programs targeting particular events, largely inhibited the emergence of a relatively independent and stable national trade campaign.

Finally, with regard to the Philippines, the SNR movement constituted an important national member of the transnational campaign: OWINFS. This international network had been engaged in crafting various mobilization techniques to oppose the WTO trade negotiation conference that was being held in Cancun in September 2003. One such method was to bring a maximum number of activists to organize protest marches at the conference venue in order to create the utmost political impact. The other method was to organize and amplify the Global Day of Action in various countries. The SNR was established with the objective of fulfilling both these objectives.

The SNR developed various strategies and action programs intent on establishing broad contacts with like-minded groups from other regions, as well as reaching out to an international audience in its efforts to illustrating the negative effects of trade liberalization on the country's economy and people's livelihoods. It also succeeded in acquiring a few of the classified documents on the government's trade negotiation positions. Travel costs for some fifteen SNR members, as well as the costs related to staff, organization of public demonstrations, media reach, a caravan protest and information diffusion inside the country were financed by different church bodies from developed countries and typically Oxfam. These funding organizations did not oppose trade liberalization processes as such, as did OWINFS. The prime concern for the first group of international campaigners was obviously related to the question of how the poorer Southern producers might favorably access the affluent Northern markets so as to help them ameliorate their general economic conditions. We have no information on how SNR internalized this tension and what effect this actually had on its work operation and effectiveness. This no doubt required the organization to maneuver carefully in its effort to cooperate with both of these international networks with divergent views.

CURRENCY TRANSACTION TAX CAMPAIGN

With respect to the area of currency transaction tax, the Argentinean case illustrated a good example of the tension in the re-appropriation of an international campaign in a given national context. An emblematical international movement like Attac was unable to make any significant impact on the national debate or at the grassroots level during the first phase of its installation in the country (between 1999 and 2001). This was the case in spite of the fact that the Argentinean national economy confronted an unprecedented crisis, including prolonged financial instabilities, capital flight, hyper-inflation and currency devaluation. In short, there existed a highly auspicious context for setting off a major popular movement around the thematic of speculative capital. This did not occur, as we have seen before, primarily because the scale of popular opposition was so elevated against the broader forms of political and economic relations that a proposition to partially tax the stock-market appeared basically "on the side" and largely inaudible.

Attac Argentina ultimately made a fundamental change in its orientation beginning from 2002 by actively joining the highly radical and popularly supported campaign against the FTAA. However, this was clearly at the cost of an internal organizational rift, thereby resulting in the founder of the movement leaving and loss of many of its original members. Most crucially, the Tobin tax issue was no longer considered to be the organization's central work program.[1] Nonetheless, such a sweeping change of orientation was also possible because the movement's local branches from their very inceptions enjoyed a great deal of autonomy in their structure, agenda setting and program implementation (Rossi 2008: 241–242).

While this new direction was being experimented, a further strain emerged with respect to the degree to which the movement should relate to the Kirchner administration. Internal followers as well as external constituencies began to express their unease about its open and growing links with the government. Indeed, many of the social movements behind the FTAA campaign, being wary of the government's ultimate compliance to international capital and financial institutions, were extremely cautious in dealing with the new administration. They feared that a close rapprochement with the public authority might affect the independence and potential of mass movements to mount autonomous campaigns. Instead they might be reduced to working in specialized committees, with the capacity to develop activities only in areas directly endorsed by the government. These kinds of debates as to whether the collective action should continue to function basically as a mobilizing factor or should also aim at elaborating and implementing concrete policy proposals in consultation with the public authorities are complex questions. The issue surfaced speedily owing to the fact that many of the powerful new government officials were previously political activists still maintaining friends and networks in civil society; yet the nature and magnitude of change proposed appeared to be modest and progressively more conciliatory towards the international financial institutions.

Attac Bolivia was a revealing case of the difficulty that an international campaign could confront in seeking to extend its core values and intervention methods to national societies. By 2001 the global Attac movement maintained national chapters in more than 25 countries, and this, too, in both the Northern and Southern countries. It acted as a galvanizing opposition against the Davos Economic Forum and played a leading role in many of the anti-globalization manifestations, including the conceiving and holding of the first major WSF in Porto Alegre in 2001. In spite of this accumulated international experience and connections, in Bolivia, its efforts completely failed. Why?

The answers are at least four-fold, according to Mayorga and Cordova. First, the Attac movement came to Bolivia through contacts established with one single person. No doubt a very righteous man (Günter Holzmann)[2] with sound contacts with the intellectual community, it was evidently not sufficient to consolidate a broad based and pungent national campaign on the currency transaction issues. Second, the Santa Cruz town where the initial campaign was launched did not have the culture of organizing massive public protests, like those in La Paz or Cochabamba, for example. Third, the proposal to install taxation on financial transactions was considered too specialized for Bolivia. Finally, Attac Bolivia sought to transpire as an omnipotent force with a grand agenda of "another world is possible." In order to push for such an ambitious program it would have needed to establish itself as an "umbrella" movement. However, this was clearly not feasible given the intense nature of mobilization that had already been taking place across many social movements and networks (Mayorga and Cordova 2008: 170–172).

Attac Bolivia had nevertheless the merit of initiating the preliminary cycle of an intense debate on the utility of financial transaction taxations for a poor country like Bolivia, activating a certain number of intellectuals and disseminating information to the parliamentarians like elsewhere. But the latter actors were concerned with more pressing political and economic problems; and the organization also did not succeed in attracting the grass roots. At the same time, the organization came with no money (unusual in a country with a long history of links with international NGOs with substantial funds), seemingly hoping that the project would take a home-grown character.

In Senegal, the idea of mobilization around the Tobin tax initiative came directly from France through contacts with the Senegalese intellectuals forming part of the wider French or European political and academic networks. At times, Attac France provided the Senegalese militants with financial supports for their regional and international travel (for example, to attend international social forums) or for printing of certain publications.[3] But such financial provisions involved only small amounts.

Apart from this distinct link, we also saw the Senegalese chapter enjoying a substantial autonomy in acclimatizing the Tobin tax question in the specific national and regional contexts. As a matter of fact, from its very inception, the issue of currency transaction did not constitute a singular or even principal activity, whereas trade liberalization, the privatization of public services and debt problems represented overriding transversal themes. Of course, this also had a negative side. One such consequence was the over-spreading of the scarce organizational resources and the lack of its ability to produce concrete impacts on any of the above fields. Second, the taking up of a host of issues meant that the leadership was often controlled by organizations maintaining specialized programs, targets and more important budget lines. This implied that Attac Senegal could not expect to have any great visibility. Overall, the movement limited itself mainly to promoting intellectual debates within the academic and informed activist circles, with little interactions with the public bodies or common people.

The international campaign to impose currency transaction tax was yet to make headways in the Philippines. As observed above, there was a degree of mobilization occurring among researchers and social organizations around the theme following the 1997 Asian financial crisis, and a number of social organizations occasionally continued to make a general reference to the potential usefulness of the currency transaction tax in the country, in particular, and South East Asia, in general. Tadem suggests that the reason for a muted national response to the international currency transaction tax campaign was due to the lack of resources available to civil society organizations (Tadem 2009c: 202). Furthermore, the radical social mobilization circle tended to reiterate that the currency transaction tax was merely a reformist proposal that could basically help preserve the capitalist system. On this last point, one could say that the currency transaction taxation initiative was not any more reformist than lets us say debt relief, anti-corruption or trade justice campaigns. The lack of finance was a valid point, and this explained partially why the organizations like the Focus on the Global South, which were initially interested in the Tobin Tax proposal, gradually moved away from this area to take on other campaign issues, notably trade justice. The point can be made that the specific choice of trade justice as a prime campaign theme was evidently related to the availability of funding in this field from international development agencies, most notably Oxfam.[4] It is noteworthy to recall that during this time the latter organization was particularly keen to link its *Make Trade Fair* campaign to dynamic national and regional movements so as to make an enhanced impact of its international advocacy.

ANTI-CORRUPTION CAMPAIGN

In Argentina, despite a widespread public concern for corruption, the establishment and consolidation of a specialized agency like the Citizen Power was possible largely as a result of the availability of external funding, mainly from the United States. Interpreting corruption as an impediment to the protection of basic human rights and promotion of a fair electoral system, the USAID and private US foundations supported its initial administrative set up. These and other foreign donor agencies also assisted the organization in the implementation of specific programs on such topics as the business participation in corruption control, public awareness raising, protection of civic rights and so forth. In fact, according to Pereyra, the contents of these first sets of programs reflected primarily the doctrine and interests of the funding agencies. The Citizen Power was able to maintain a leeway merely in naming the programs differently suiting the national context. In general, it developed and implemented anti-corruption projects as per the objective and anticipation of the funding organizations without any capacity to altering their conceptual contents (Pereyra 2008: 101–102).

From the mid-1990s onwards, the Citizen Power began to conduct research, create databanks, conceive specialized publications and utilize national media in a more professional fashion. The organization carried out surveys to gauge public opinion on the perceived nature and extent of corruption in the country; it looked at the unscrupulous practice prevalent within the country's judiciary system; and it participated in the monitoring of the fair conduct of elections and engagement in unlawful activities by political parties. Accordingly, the organization started to recruit younger people with more specialized skills. This was fitting to foreign funding agencies' general requirements as well, since the creation of a reliable data source on corruption were readily sought after internationally (for example for the TI's creation of the annual corruption perception indices), and the proficiently prepared project proposals and analytical documents were important instruments to obtain additional funding. One outcome of this evolution was that the organization progressively transformed itself into a professional NGO with a relatively a large administrative structure and budget, as well as a stable program of action. The result was an ever increased organizational demand and a subsequent acute dependency on foreign financial sources.

In Bolivia, much of the corruption control measures was designed primarily to fulfill the country's international obligation to implement the major corruption conventions (as such formally signed by the Bolivian government). They were also directly linked to the attempt by the USAID and US private foundations to promote projects aimed at achieving greater integrity and transparency in public life. Thus, both the essential conception of corruption and necessary financial resources came directly from abroad, with a little genuine participation from the Bolivian civil society. As a matter of fact, unlike Argentine, even such activities as the collection of basic data and carrying out of research surveys on corruption were frequently handled by foreign experts or institutions. For example, the USAID, the principal funding agency for corruption control measures in the country, used the American management consultancy firm Casals & Associates for mapping out local perceptions on corruption (Mayorga and Cordova 2008: 151–152).

Within civil society organizations and movements (often dominated by labor unions, production cooperatives and left-wing parties) the condemnation of corruption was very much a part of the general discourse against the ruling political class or foreign domination in the economic sphere. In recent years, the occurrence of corruption has been attributed mainly to the consequence of a growing influence of the neoliberal economic dogma. As a result, whatever limited concrete initiatives that occurred around the corruption control issues tended to come mainly from the former state officials or young professionals rather than from the activists associated with trade unions or similar social movements. Widely travelled and connected to the international donor circle, these retired functionaries, together with the young dynamic people freshly graduated often with a good English level, also possessed many of the professional requirements sought after by the foreign agencies funding projects on corruption control measures.

In Senegal, the case of FC was most revealing in terms of knowing how an international anti-corruption campaign organization like the TI could influence the national agenda so decisively. Whether its general vision, objectives, strategy or specific intervention programs, the FC was completely inspired, if not completely induced, by the TI. On the other hand, the FC, too, "benefited greatly from this affiliation which gave it a greater visibility and credibility to its local project," especially "against the repressive tendencies of local political power" (Thioub 2007: 42). Apart from this, the FC was also able to make use of the TI's recognition and contacts for considerably expanding its financial support base. As a matter of fact, several new anti-corruption projects were added in its work programs with grants from the USAID, Soros Foundations Networks, International Development Research Centre, Friedrich Naumann Foundation, and the European Union.[5] Naturally, by providing financial assistance, these agencies greatly modeled the strategic orientation and substance of the specific programs that were being implemented by the organization. On the other hand, such financial supports were particularly decisive for its day-to-day functioning as well as long-term survival in the face of a generalized indifference to the phenomenon of corruption on the part of the government authorities as well as the common citizens, as was noted earlier.

Turning now to the Philippines, although the occurrence of bribery and fraud were commonly recognized as a serious problem by the general public and the government, as well as frequently covered in the press, the availability of outside ideas and resources were the primary motivation to crafting a coherent national campaign in this area.[6] The TAN, the principal anti-corruption national organization, despite attesting a certain degree of its capacity to mobilize various social actors, took on board the principles of "accountability," "transparency" and "good governance" bolstered energetically by such agencies as the World Bank, USAID and UNDP, without linking these dimensions to the structural political and societal conditions that frequently generated corruption. The reasons for this were rather straightforward: these leading donor agencies made readily available important sources of funds to national organizations, notably the TAN, to formulate and implement various project based anti-corruption initiatives. The fact that the national corruption agenda was propelled by these conformist development agencies also explained why the anti-corruption campaign in the Philippines did not assume any anti-neoliberal discourse, unlike the trade justice or debt relief movements, for example.

Summarized succinctly, the previous discussion shows rather clearly that the source and significance of influence resided markedly on the international campaign groups. We may emphasize at least two dimensions here: the command over campaign ideas and financial resources. Concerning the first component, no doubt themes of debt relief, trade liberalization, anti-corruption, and, to a limited extent, the financial speculation and taxation matters were not completely unfamiliar at the national level, but the international groups possessed infinitely more ideas on what was being discussed at the global level, the specific events that could be targeted for mobilization efforts and how certain conceptions and propositions could be prioritized (further details on this will be provided in part 4). Only once all these aspects comprehended and the related actions were planned, the global message would come down to the lower level in the form of communication or as calls for wider participation by national social organizations.

In this, certain campaigns were more directive than others though. For example, much of the corruption ideas and structuring of specific campaigns tended to come directly from Europe or North America in a very preconceived and hierarchical fashion. In other words, the headquarters, key specialists and central ideas for projects development were located essentially in the North. Regarding the trade justice campaign, the agencies such as Oxfam descended to the national level in order to make their international campaigns more effective, but the important point here is that such campaigns were already devised and elaborated at their headquarters. Typically, the prime role left for national collaborating organizations was rather to faithfully implement these activities. Likewise, the idea to push forward a consolidated worldwide movement for debt forgiveness in the late 1990s had emerged at the international level, impelled by international Christian charity organizations conspicuously in response to the Jubilee 2000 celebration activities. What is interesting in this respect is that, undoubtedly quite radical in its overall perception to the present world economic structure, the Attac movement, too, did not differ in any significant manner in this realm. The initial idea for greater public regulation or taxing of financial markets was first conceived in Paris by the French or European intellectuals and attempts were subsequently made to popularize the campaign in different countries and regions by utilizing leftwing academic networks and parliamentarians.

In regards to the issue of financial resources, we found no trace of national groups financing international campaign activities. On the other hand, the transnational campaigns seeking to expand their influence came to the national level characteristically with funds to support the set up of national counterpart organizations or put into practice their main campaign activities. At times this provided much needed resources for national dynamics, but ultimately most national organizations ended up being in a critically dependent position. Even those national organizations that could have potentially mobilized their constituencies to achieve a greater degree of financial autonomy (based for example on membership contributions) began to rely on foreign assistance for cash requirements and expanding activities, thereby becoming gradually reduced to designing programs to suit, primarily, their international counterparts. The availability of international funds in the end became the major criteria for adhering to a specific international campaign. This explains why Oxfam was able to widely mobilize national activists in a regular manner, while the Attac movement was progressively sidelined. The truth is that in certain cases, the national social organizations which were initially attracted by intellectual content and vivaciousness of Attac's global campaign switched their efforts to other campaigns once it became clear that this movement had little or no financial resources to offer. As we observed above, this was particularly the case in the Philippines.

The consequence of an acute international dependency for essential campaign ideas and financial resources meant that, by and large, no stable and autonomous organizational structure could develop at the national level. Even where a certain number of potent national organizations emerged, they were required to make constant shifts in ideas, time frames, strategic focus and specific program activities, depending upon the international requirement and resources availability. Besides, most of the actions planned at the international level tended to be fairly short term. This was for the simple reason that a good number of activities planned at the international level were event-based (for example, getting organized around a particular world conference), thus generally requiring only occasional cooperation from the national level. This was the case even with the transnational corruption movement (which held by and large the most stable organizational structure) as the framing of campaign activities based on international debates and events tended to result in a cyclical national funding situation and at times making national activists further exposed to legal and political prosecutions by powerful fraudulent political and business elites. In a nutshell, the sporadic nature of planning of activities at the international level implied difficulties in consolidating a solid organizational base for a durable and structured domestic social action. Taken together, there was a general marginality of national structures within the overall organizational configuration of all four transnational campaigns.

NOTES

1. This sort of discord regarding whether the movement should stay faithful to the original mandate of the movement, the promotion of currency transaction taxation, or become more active in popular mobilizations by seeking to pull the movement towards broader social processes and events was not unique to Argentina, since a similar outcome took place in France, too (see Morena 2007: 31–36).

2. He has generally been admired as "the spiritual father" of both the Attac and WSF movements in the country (*El Deber* June 2, 2001).

3. See, for example, Attac France. http://www.france.attac.org/spip.php? articles8326 (accessed September 14, 2009).

4. Indeed, Oxfam Great Britain, together with its sister agency Novib in the Netherlands, remained a key initial donor for the whole of the Focus on the Global South operations (personal interview with the organization's direction, Walden Bello, Nairobi, January 2007).

5. Senegalese Social Forum, http://www.forumcivil.sn/spip.php?article1 (accessed September 14, 2009).

6. The situation in which civil society associations become directly intertwined with outside resources and interests have long been recognized in the Philippines, as Hedman, for example, notes concerning the national democratic movement as a whole during and after the Marcos autocratic regime: "The identity and internal solidity of these secondary associations evolved over time in sync with the changing resources and interests of this dominant bloc in the Philippines and in tandem with shifting transnational linkages and international conditions" (Hedman 2006: 178).

III

WORLD SOCIAL FORUM

4

Basic Values and Organizational Configuration

As a transnational social movement, the World Social Forum (WSF) stands out to be a noteworthy case. It has attained a remarkable growth. It is probably difficult to find a transnational social movement in the past that saw as rapid expansion and renown as the WSF. But there are also other attributes associated with its basic values and organizational structure that testify the distinctiveness of the movement.

The WSF's origin goes back to the continued intellectual contacts and exchanges among the academics and activists on the left, despite their general ideological disorientation following the collapse of the Soviet Union and vigorous adherence of China to open liberal economy. At the same time, market economy, as a single dominant model at the global level, was far from free of reproach. On the contrary, the negative effects of the ultraliberal economic policies spearheaded by the British Prime Minister Madam Thatcher and United States President Regan in the 1980s were becoming increasingly palpable with the growing incidence of poverty and inequality in many contexts. At the same time, the essential public services were gradually downsized or privatized.

These outcomes created a significant opening for scholarly discussions and militant activities. Sociologists like Bourdieu asserted that the market was functioning outside democratic control. As such, institutional regulations on the part of the State as well as the political pressure from social organizations were considered necessary for regulating the market economy (Bourdieu 2001: 16).

During the 1990s, the debates on the nature and functioning of the free market economy, particularly its negative consequences, became particularly intense in Europe. Many fundamental mutations in international economy were occurring at a time when Europe was engaged in the creation of the world's most powerful economic community. Academics, trade unionist leaders and political personalities from the left-wing and green political parties argued that the liberal economic model was steadily destroying the "social acquisitions" in Europe, while at the same time causing intolerable mistreatment of people and the environment worldwide. A certain degree of support to this line of thinking also came from the traditional social democratic parties, which considered that basic social norms and human values should not be undermined in promoting the singular economic logic of productivity and deregulation. In France, *Le monde diplomatique* and the Attac movement remained deeply engaged in organizing critical intellectual debates and popular manifestations, insisting that a political ideology that cared for the protection of social rights and wider working class interest was still pertinent and legitimate.

Within this perspective, we see the emergence of a new form of thinking and conducting of political actions. We may note here two developments. First, there was an attempt to move away from the idea of bringing significant social and political changes through the leadership of a vanguard party. The approach gave pre-eminence to network politics, recognizing particularly the efficacy of social organizations and actions based on the aggregation of diverse forces. Concurrently, an increasing emphasis was placed on the utilization of new information technology, particularly the Internet.

Second, there was a strong influence of the concept of "multitudes," advanced by Negri and Hardt. These authors suggested that the "Empire," embedded in the contemporary processes of globalization, was not only increasingly de-legitimated, but it also triggered off many creative forms of cooperation and collaboration across nations and continents, including innumerable encounters (Hardt and Negri 2004:7). Away from conceiving of social actions based primarily on the "people," "masses" or "working classes," they argued that the notion of "a social multiplicity" allowed an enhanced prospect "to communicate and act jointly while maintaining their internal differences" (ibid. 8).

Naturally, both these approaches were closely associated with the attempt by scholars to adapt Marxism (as an ideology as well as practice) to a new evolving international political, economic and cultural context.

This is a broad account of the history of the rise of the alternative globalization movement now commonly known within most academic and social movements' circles. In this regard, what needs to be underlined is that, as the general critique and reflection against the liberal economic model and its functioning advanced, conceiving of some form of an organizational structure to maintain the momentum going transpired to be an obvious necessity. The creation of the WSF was in many ways the direct result of this realization. As a matter of fact, the WSF emerged not only as a primary organizational set up of the alternative globalization movement but also as a specific experimental case in transnational network politics_ thus built in on the philosophical tenets of the "multitudes."

Established in Geneva in February 2000 with the leading impulse of the French and (francophone) Brazilian intellectuals, the first international Social Forum took place in the southeastern Brazilian city of Porto Alegre in January 2001. This host-city was led by a labor party mayor with a significant experience in formulating city management plans based on the notion and practice of "participatory budget."[1] In addition to this, according to De Paula, the Brazilian civil society organizations, notably the Brazilian Forum of NGOs and Social Movements (FBOMS[2]), had acquired, from the time of the United Nations Rio conference on the environment and development in 1992, many relevant skills in handling the fundamental logistical matters in organizing major international gatherings. The leading Brazilian civil society actors were particularly adept in establishing a dynamic and gainful working relationship with the government, an element considered utterly vital in successfully holding these sorts of meetings. More importantly, they commenced to cherish the idea that as globalization processes concerned all people, it was fundamental that the plurality of actors and diversity of topics were promoted in these kinds of international public forums (De Paula 2006: 99).

AN INSTANTANEOUS SUCCESS

In any event, the experimentation of the WSF proved to be an immediate success. What made this possible? Two factors are worth mentioning. First, the WSF demonstrated capacity to bring together many influential social movements. The minimum denominator for these movements to come together was their common opposition to the neoliberal economic policies promoted by the leading international financial and commercial institutions. Added to this was their shared concern about the growing and largely uninhibited worldwide operation of powerful multinational companies with severe negative consequences for the protection of basic human rights and the local environment. Likewise, they commonly expressed antagonism against the political hegemonic role of the United States in world affairs, notably following its invasion of Iraq in 2003. Brazil's powerful landless peoples' movement (MST[3]), worldwide agrarian network Via Campesina, the movement of Indians in Chiapas, the Attac movement in Europe and trade union federations in North America and elsewhere swiftly became the key enthusiastic allies of the WSF. Although started with the lead of francophone intellectuals as stated above, many Anglophone academics and international development NGOs (notably Oxfam) were soon to join the movement. The WSF could also count on the backing and protection of the left and green political parties in Europe. Moreover, social democratic parties in several countries (particularly in Scandinavia) and numerous Christian charity outfits lent their support to the movement. This explains why these latter organizations (represented by themselves or the organizations that they sponsor) have remained so overwhelmingly perceptible at most global and regional social forums. On the whole, the support provided to the WSF by varieties of networks of social movements, political parties and NGOs was most critical for both gaining a wide degree of political legitimacy as well as securing financial assistance for the basic functioning of the movement.

Second, the movement was able to bring together a considerable number of people at its global forums. Let us highlight this with some figures. With the initial number of 4,700 participants in 2001, this annual event gathered 113,000 people in 2009. And in 2003, it assembled as many as 155,000 persons (see Table 1). The reason for this noticeably high participation in 2003 was three-fold: (a) a socially and economically explosive national context, notably in South American countries such as Argentina, Bolivia, as well as Brazil, (b) a wide-ranging regional and international opposition to the United States unilateral decision to intervene in Iraq in 2003, and (c) the event was coincided with the launching of the FATT under the active leadership of the United States government which many social organizations and movements opted to actively oppose for various reasons as was seen in the previous discussion.

Table 1.   The Number of People Participating in Global Social Forums, 2001–2010

Year	Place	Number of registered participants
2001	Porto Alegre	4,700
2002	Porto Alegre	12,274
2003	Porto Alegre	27,763
2004	Mumbai	74,126
2005	Porto Alegre	155,000
2006	Bamako	10,000
	Caracas	53,000
	Karachi	30,000
2007	Nairobi	75,000
2008	No international or regional forums were organized	
2009	Belem	113,000
2010	No international or regional forums were organized	

Source: WSF. http://www.forumsocialmundial.org.br/main.php?id_menu=14&cd_language=2 (accessed January 10, 2010); WSF. http://www.forumsocialmundial.org.br/noticias_01.php?cd_news=2556&cd_language=2 (accessed January 10, 2010).

In addition to the international forums, many regional and national social forums were organized mobilizing a considerable number of people. In certain regions such as in Europe, the earlier regional forums held in Florence (2002), Paris (2003) and London (2004) attracted a large attendance of unemployed people, students, immigrants, academics, media people and political party representatives. Evidently these decentralized forums offered the possibilities of considering concrete national and regional problems. For example, the 6th European social forum, organized in July 2010 in Istanbul, took place in a context of an acute world financial crisis and the social, political and environmental consequences of the wars in Iraq and Afghanistan led by the United States. Besides evoking these fundamental international relations dimensions, the meeting lucidly reminded the Turkish national context marked by frequent human rights violations, political conflicts involving minority groups such as the Kurdish people, the gender question, implications of the growing economic investments by multinational, European and large national business companies and many severe environmental degradation problems commonly experienced in different parts of the country in recent years.

In these global, regional and national forums, in addition to the holding of protest marches and popular gatherings, the organizers regularly called for searching out "alternatives." They emphasized that analyzing the situation or simply criticizing the "system" was not adequate. Numerous workshops, small as well as quite large, were organized to hammer out different propositions. Even though the organization in the end attempted neither to recapitulate nor called for any implementation of these propositions, the importance given to the practical aspect of social activism was clearly worthy of note. As a matter of fact, from its inception, it was this particular facet that made the WSF to stand out as a distinct constituent within the alternative globalization movement.

A NEW CULTURE OF MOBILIZATION

Following the successful organization of the first international social forum in Porto Alegre in January 2001, the organization committee constituting some eight Brazilian social organizations went ahead and prepared a Charter of Principles governing the movement's core principles and methods of functioning (Figure 3). This document was subsequently widely approved by social movements outside of Brazil. Sketched out in 14 articles, the Charter of Principles highlighted the movement's deep commitment to finding a new culture of working and mobilizing of popular forces. One dimension of this new culture was the attempt to transform the movement into "a permanent process of seeking and building alternatives" (Article 2). Behind this idea of working towards concrete proposals, it also laid its effort to prove that the WSF or the alternative globalization movement in general was no longer a simple gathering platform of "irresponsible left-wingers,"[4] but instead it was a reservoir of ideas that policy makers themselves could readily utilize. These ideas commonly encompassed the questions of world peace, democracy, solidarity, environmental preservation, poverty reduction, strengthening of the multilateral system, and so forth to which many governments, as well as by broad-minded political organizations, the Churches, trade unions and development NGOs could easily consent. Consequently, the Charter stipulated that the movement remained "open to pluralism and to the diversity of activities and ways of engaging" (Article 9).

FIGURE 3.   WORLD SOCIAL
FORUM CHARTER OF PRINCIPLES

The committee of Brazilian organizations that conceived of, and organized, the first World Social Forum, held in Porto Alegre from January 25th to 30th, 2001, after evaluating the results of that Forum and the expectations it raised, consider it necessary and legitimate to draw up a Charter of Principles to guide the continued pursuit of that initiative. While the principles contained in this Charter—to be respected by all those who wish to take part in the process and to organize new editions of the World Social Forum—are a consolidation of the decisions that presided over the holding of the Porto Alegre Forum and ensured its success, they extend the reach of those decisions and define orientations that flow from their logic.

1. The World Social Forum is an open meeting place for reflective thinking, democratic debate of ideas, formulation of proposals, free exchange of experiences and interlinking for effective action, by groups and movements of civil society that are opposed to neo-liberalism and to domination of the world by capital and any form of imperialism, and are committed to building a planetary society directed towards fruitful relationships among Humankind and between it and the Earth.

2. The World Social Forum at Porto Alegre was an event localized in time and place. From now on, in the certainty proclaimed at Porto Alegre that "another world is possible," it becomes a permanent process of seeking and building alternatives, which cannot be reduced to the events supporting it.

3. The World Social Forum is a world process. All the meetings that are held as part of this process have an international dimension.

4. The alternatives proposed at the World Social Forum stand in op-position to a process of globalization commanded by the large mul-tinational corporations and by the governments and international institutions at the service of those corporations' interests, with the complicity of national governments. They are designed to ensure that globalization in solidarity will prevail as a new stage in world history. This will respect universal human rights, and those of all citizens—men and women—of all nations and the environment and will rest on democratic international systems and institutions at the service of social justice, equality and the sovereignty of peoples.

5. The World Social Forum brings together and interlinks only orga-nizations and movements of civil society from all the countries in the world, but it does not intend to be a body representing world civil society.

6. The meetings of the World Social Forum do not deliberate on be-half of the World Social Forum as a body. No one, therefore, will be authorized, on behalf of any of the editions of the Forum, to express positions claiming to be those of all its participants. The participants in the Forum shall not be called on to take decisions as a body, whether by vote or acclamation, on declarations or propos-als for action that would commit all, or the majority, of them and that propose to be taken as establishing positions of the Forum as a body. It thus does not constitute a locus of power to be disputed by the participants in its meetings, nor does it intend to constitute the only option for interrelation and action by the organizations and movements that participate in it.

7. Nonetheless, organizations or groups of organizations that partici-pate in the Forums meetings must be assured the right, during such meetings, to deliberate on declarations or actions they may decide on, whether singly or in coordination with other participants. The World Social Forum undertakes to circulate such decisions widely by the means at its disposal, without directing, hierarchizing, cen-suring or restricting them, but as deliberations of the organizations or groups of organizations that made the decisions.

8. The World Social Forum is a plural, diversified, non-confessional, non-governmental and non-party context that, in a decentralized fashion, interrelates organizations and movements engaged in concrete action at levels from the local to the international to build another world.

9. The World Social Forum will always be a forum open to plural-ism and to the diversity of activities and ways of engaging of the organizations and movements that decide to participate in it, as

well as the diversity of genders, ethnicities, cultures, generations and physical capacities, providing they abide by this Charter of Principles. Neither party representations nor military organizations shall participate in the Forum. Government leaders and members of legislatures who accept the commitments of this Charter may be invited to participate in a personal capacity.

10. The World Social Forum is opposed to all totalitarian and reductionist views of economy, development and history and to the use of violence as a means of social control by the State. It upholds respect for Human Rights, the practices of real democracy, participatory democracy, peaceful relations, in equality and solidarity, among people, ethnicities, genders and peoples, and condemns all forms of domination and all subjection of one person by another.

11. As a forum for debate, the World Social Forum is a movement of ideas that prompts reflection, and the transparent circulation of the results of that reflection, on the mechanisms and instruments of domination by capital, on means and actions to resist and overcome that domination, and on the alternatives proposed to solve the problems of exclusion and social inequality that the process of capitalist globalization with its racist, sexist and environmentally destructive dimensions is creating internationally and within countries.

12. As a framework for the exchange of experiences, the World Social Forum encourages understanding and mutual recognition among its participant organizations and movements, and places special value on the exchange among them, particularly on all that society is building to center economic activity and political action on meeting the needs of people and respecting nature, in the present and for future generations.

13. As a context for interrelations, the World Social Forum seeks to strengthen and create new national and international links among organizations and movements of society, that—in both public and private life—will increase the capacity for non-violent social resistance to the process of dehumanization the world is undergoing and to the violence used by the State, and reinforce the humanizing measures being taken by the action of these movements and organizations.

14. The World Social Forum is a process that encourages its participant organizations and movements to situate their actions, from the local level to the national level and seeking active participation in international contexts, as issues of planetary citizenship,

and to introduce onto the global agenda the change-inducing practices that they are experimenting in building a new world in solidarity.

Approved and adopted in São Paulo, on April 9, 2001, by the organizations that make up the World Social Forum Organizing Committee, approved with modifications by the World Social Forum International Council on June 10, 2001.

Source: WSF. http://www.forumsocialmundial.org.br/main.php?id_menu= 4&cd_language=2 (accessed January 10, 2010).

By far the most significant feature outlined in the Charter was the movement's rejection of violence as a way of brining about important social transformations (article 10). As such, it abstained from calling for taking up arms to overturn the system that would ultimately have led to major sacrifices, including bloodshed, among participating individuals and organizations. At the same time, a strict compliance to the principle of peaceful methods meant that the WSF could remove the peril of the movement being potentially influenced by radical or armed groups. Accordingly, the WSF ardently advocated persuasive methods based on popular mobilization, rallying of public opinion, media coverage as well as constructing of alliances with progressive governments and more open-minded international organizations (such as the United Nations system). For this reason, precisely, the Charter regarded the WSF as "an open meeting place for reflective thinking, democratic debate of ideas, formulation of proposals, free exchange of experiences and interlinking for effective action by groups and movements of civil society" (Article 1).

One further characteristic of the Charter was its belief in broad humanist values (Ghimire, forthcoming). It described, for example, that the groups and movements represented within the WSF were "committed to building a planetary society directed towards fruitful relationships among Humankind and between it and the Earth. This will respect universal human rights, and those of all citizens—men and women—of all nations and the environment and will rest on democratic international systems and institutions at the service of social justice, equity and the sovereignty of peoples" (Article 4). Overall, the Charter advanced series of demands intended for ameliorating the living conditions of the average lot, democratic deficits, world peace and ecological protections, in addition to its emphasis on the non-violent and persuasive methods, as we noted above. Undoubtedly, many of these elements constituted vital humanist ideals.

ORGANIZATIONAL STRUCTURE

The Charter viewed the WSF as "a permanent process of seeking and building alternatives" (Article 2) with "an international dimension" (Article 3). This suggested that the movement aimed at maintaining a durable organizational configuration. It also aimed at operating at the global level. But how was this to be actually structured and managed?

According to the Charter, the WSF was an effort to "bring together" and "interlink" the various "organizations and movements of civil society from all the countries in the world" (Article 5). Yet, the text did not specify what these organizations and movements were and how they were to be selected, considering that innumerable organizations (good as well as bad) would exist within civil society. Even among the righteous types of organizations, there could be no guarantee that all of them would necessarily agree to the organizational procedures foreseen in the current arrangements. In the same way, the Charter did not spell out how and under what conditions these various organizations or movements might be coalesced and interconnected.

The Charter did specify one thing though: among these organizations and movements, no single entity was endorsed to claim to have represented the WSF. Nor was it "authorized, on behalf of any of the editions of the Forum, to express positions claiming to be those of all its participants" (Article 6). The Charter also specified that "the participants in the Forum shall not be called on to take decisions as a body, whether by vote or acclamation, or declarations or proposals for action that would commit all, or the majority, of them" (ibid.). Evidently, the consideration behind this was that the WSF did not "constitute a locus of power to be disputed by the participants in its meetings" (ibid.).

Nevertheless, for a worldwide initiative of this nature, the existence of a certain form of organizational structure was clearly unavoidable. Beyond any doubt, the holding of an international meeting of several thousand participants in a regular manner was not a simple affair. A certain form of an organizational body became necessary to conceive and organize the event, as well as maintain the follow-up of this undertaking. Furthermore, this required a considerable amount of coordination and communication. The question is therefore how were these activities handled within the WSF?

In an effort to answer this question, we may begin by noting the existence of the movement's central office (designated as the Secretariat) in Sao Paulo. Somewhat a small body with three full-time staff, its prime responsibility was to facilitate the contacts between various organizations and movements involved with the holding of social forums at various levels. Logically, it served as a source of information and public relations body at the international level.[5] On the whole, its primary function was limited to maintaining indispensable activities such as the keeping of records, dispatching of information and other similar aspects related to the basic internal administrative operation of the movement.

The Brazilian Organizing Committee (OC) functioned as an important entity within the WSF's organizational structure. This body organized the international social forums in 2001, 2002, 2003, 2005 and 2009 in Brazil and continued to closely interact with its counterpart organizations in Mumbai in 2004, in Bamako, Caracas and Karachi in 2006 and in Nairobi in 2007. The body was created in 2001 with eight Brazilian civil society organizations, but this number increased to 23 organizations in 2005. This numerical aspect apart, what seemed especially important was the nature and standing of many of these social organizations within the Brazilian society. For example, we find in this committee the central Association of Brazilian NGOs (ABONG[6]), a leading trade union movement CUT (*Central Unica dos Trabalhadores*), the MST rural landless workers movement, a major human rights organization like the Social Network of Justice and Human Rights (RSJDH[7]), important Christian charity bodies deeply impregnated by liberation theology viewpoints such as the Brazilian Commission of Justice and Peace (CBJP[8]) and a political think tank body with important international connections like the Brazilian Institute of Social and Economic Analysis (IBASE[9]). The combined strength of these social organizations was that all major WSF events could be successfully organized. Naturally, this gave these organizations pre-eminence both inside and outside of the country, as well as a certain degree of legitimacy in their effort to assert sway over the entire WSF movement.

Likewise, national and regional organizing committees were set up for Asia, Africa, Latin America, as well as North America and Europe, albeit with a greatly varying mobilization capacity. For example, the Indian National Committee responsible for organizing the 2004 World Social Forum in Mumbai has continued to demonstrate a certain degree of weight within the WSF organizational chain of command. On the contrary, the Kenya national committee which organized the 2007 World Social Forum has been able to exert no or very little influence. As for the regional committees, the European Social Forum has remained a particularly potent force, as noted earlier. It has organized several enthusiastic social forums invoking many pertinent European and global economic and political questions. Indeed, as we will see subsequently, this body has also been able to greatly mold both much of the strategy and activities of the central WSF movement, and this, too, ever since its very inception. The North American regional organizing committee, too, has demonstrated a certain degree of mobilization capacity.

The International Council (IC) has remained by far the most powerful body within the WSF organizational structure. A permanent organ, it has been composed of the Brazilian organizing committee, Indian and Kenyan national organizing committees, many members of the European regional organizing committee, the North American trade union movements, and so forth. Furthermore, several powerful international NGOs, especially equipped with reliable internal budgets, useful contacts and networks have been represented as IC members. Functioning since June 2001, this organ has the overall responsibility of defining the movements' fundamental strategic and operational matters, notably involving the following activities:

- "Formulating WSF strategies
- Maintaining ongoing contact with international movements, campaigns, initiatives, struggles and other events
- Making the WSF a familiar presence in their countries and regions, fostering widespread participation and debate on matters and proposals identified by the WSF
- Promoting and supporting WSF meetings, identifying potential sites and encouraging participation
- Ensuring reciprocal political, thematic and operational action among WSFs
- Promoting and supporting the formation of Committees in their countries
- Together with WSF Organizing Committees, providing a structure for topics, methodologies, formats, identification and invitations to speakers and exhibitors
- Fund-raising"[10]

In order to carry out these tasks in a more concerted manner, from 2003 on, the IC created under its leadership six specialized commissions:

1. Strategic commission to guide the new and long-term orientations of the movement
2. Content commission with the task of collecting essential material emerging from the different forums, organizing this information by themes and disseminating it to the WSF participants
3. Methodology commission to ensure that the "open" nature of the WSF and plurality of actors are maintained
4. Expansion commission with the purpose of enhancing the development of regional, national and local forums
5. Communication commission for an improved dissemination of information on the WSF processes both within the movement and outside
6. Finance commission to identify different sources of funds so as to cover the growing costs for the WSF activities[11]

The IC met regularly, often coinciding with the holding of a major regional or international forum. In these meetings, the organizational dimension of the upcoming world social forum, particularly the selection (or non-selection) of a specific country or region for hosting of a particular international social forum,[12] was the principal matter commonly dealt with. In addition to this, the IC supervised the setting up of social forum organizing committees in countries hosting major WSF events, including the assessment regarding the indispensible logistics and financial questions.

In these meetings, numerous critical questions were often raised and discussed concerning the overall political strategic direction of the movement. For example, in its meeting in February 2009 in Belem, heated debates took place among participating delegates on the issue of the political coherence of the movement. Certain participants thought that there was an overwhelming fragmentation in mobilization efforts. They believed the WSF lacked close contacts with social actors, movements and struggles at the grassroots level. In particular, they expressed uneasiness about the growing domination of powerful international NGOs over the movement.[13]

In some ways, these debates reflected the different political sensitivities of the participating delegates, namely, between those viewing the WSF primarily as a space for regular meetings, contacts and the exchange of different experiences among social organizations opposing the neoliberal policies and related consequences and those who wanted to use it as a springboard for mounting worldwide collective and radical actions (see on this debate, for example, Whitaker 2006:126). In general, the former stance tended to prevail within the organization. This is in part because this position was strongly favored by the Brazilian Organizing Committee (hence the original and fundamental pillar behind the institutionalization of the WSF process) and by politically moderate yet financially well-endowed international NGOs (which were naturally very much concerned about the risk of losing their control of the movement in the event of its unwarranted radicalization). Related to this, ironically, the IC's practice of taking decisions with consensus among those present helped the more powerful element of the movement to impose their overall will. According to Whitaker, this system was meant to provide the strong as well as weaker groups with a sort of right of veto. However, in practice "the strongest ones have generally tended to utilize this power" (Whitaker 2006: 125).

ORGANIZATIONAL AND MOBILIZATION POTENCY

Against the background of these complexities, a continued unease existed between the need to have to make the movement functional by achieving a certain degree of organizational stability and the movement's governing Charter that disallowed the presence of leaders or the formulation of any binding resolutions. This implied that no spokesperson or decisions came out in the open public arena. An ultimate result of this situation was the emergence of a considerable degree of ambiguity within much of the WSF's organizational and decision-making structure.

In the same way, as the movement assembled a large spectrum of geographically and ideologically varying groups, taking or implementing prompt decisions on urgent organizational and mobilizational matters became extremely complicated. Again, according to the Charter, the WSF was "a plural, diversified, non-confessional, non-governmental and non-party context that, in a decentralized fashion, interrelates organizations and movements engaged in concrete action at levels from local to the international" (Article 8). Let us imagine that the IC truthfully cared for taking important decisions in line with these principles of inclusiveness and decentralization. This would obviously have required the IC to go through a significant consultative process involving the national, regional and continental organization committees, as well as to ensure the representation and plurality of views of these units. Such an objective would have been distinctly arduous and ambitious.

Already some scholars believed that the need to have to mobilize forces for conceiving and organizing of numerous social forums from local, national, regional and global hampered the overall dynamics of the movement by dispersing resources and organizational energy (Jervolino et al., 2008: 27). Furthermore, given that the prevailing linkages and interactions between center and bases at the local, national and regional levels were more or less voluntary, there was obviously little guarantee that the different decisions, recommendations and appeals coming from the IC could automatically be implemented by every one. Discernibly, many these social organizations confronted numerous financial, staff, office infrastructure constraints; as such, they were obliged to remain attentive, first of all, to their own requirements and activities before taking on extra responsibilities. Taken as a whole, the WSF's organizational structure could be qualified as exceptionally burdensome and blurred.

Significantly, a given group or organization could join and abandon the overarching movement on its own will. This was even more so with individuals as they could freely chose to rally with the movement only at a specific moment or for a specific action. In the absence of a membership-based structure, the followers or sympathizers had no particular liability or allegiance to the organization. In other words, they retained the full freedom as to when and the degree to which they would want to support the movement. In particular, the participation in international forums often implied important sacrifices on their time and financial resources. The potential participants or activists therefore needed to weigh up if the costs borne were worth the expected gains by attending these meetings, unless their travel expenses were covered by the WSF or other funding agencies. The likely benefits by participating in the WSF meeting included an enhanced exposure to the experiences from other regions, increased exchange of information with other movements, salutary contacts with international civil society networks and potential funding sources and the possibility of publicizing their own work. However, accessing these gains was far from automatic. Also, not all of them could hope to draw benefits in a similar manner.

Owing to the fact that the WSF was extremely wary about the influence of political parties, the movement notably lacked a crucial "political instrument" for trying to channel its propositions to the more practical public arena (for example through the utilization of political parties; see on this aspect Sehm-Patomaki and Ulvila, 2006: 180–186). For that reason, the movement faced a major structural difficulty in seeking to implement its salient propositions. Nor could it expect to yield any direct impacts in concrete contexts.

Over the years, with the holding of numerous large popular forums at various levels, the movement steadily took a "gigantic" form. In particular, the organization of an international forum each year with the mobilization of a maximum number of participants was seen as the essential political strategy of the movement. Given that its declared objective was to countering the Davos Economic Forum, this approach was nearly imperative. However, this situation tended to create an enormous burden to the organization, with the key individuals and groups behind the movement constantly running to ensure the basic logistical items (e.g., dealing with local/national authorities, organizing meeting facilities, security inspections, transport facilities, etc.) rather than being able to fully participate in the public debates and general mobilization activities. These types of global conferences have usually proven difficult affairs even for the large international United Nations agencies with a strong organizational setup and the provision of financial contributions by member countries (Ghimire 2010: 1–21). Evidently, the WSF possessed no such resources; and on top of this, its informal organization structure and a highly inflexible nature of its Charter made it extremely difficult to continually cope with the growth and enormousness of the different initiatives that were being undertaken. Taken as a whole, there was clearly a profound tension between the desire to incessantly amplify the movement's activities and its visibility and its limited organizational and resources capacity.

One direct consequence of this gigantic nature of the movement was that the costs for organizing national, regional and international forums constantly amplified.[14] At the same time, the movement's income levels did not match the growing needs created by the increase in activities and participants. Evidence suggests that, between 2001 and 2005, the total income of the movement rose from 1.65 million USD to 8.27 million USD. However, the expenditure (based on the anticipation of income) remained persistently higher. This led to a chronic deficit, rising by more than 1.5 million USD in 2005.[15] As a result, no international forum could be organized in 2006; and in 2007, financial difficulties compelled the organizers of the Nairobi global social forum to seek sponsorships from multinational hotel chains and telephone companies, thereby attracting a great deal of criticism from within the movement.[16] Similarly, due primarily to a severe financial difficulty, the 2010 edition of the WSF international forum was called off.

NOTES

1. The notion of the "participatory budget" calls for a direct engagement of the population at the local (municipal) level in different phases of budget preparation and implementation with the concern of defining priorities and resources allocation by itself (cf. rather than by politicians or technicians) (see, for example, Abers 1998: 512–537).

2. *Fórum Brasileiro de ONGs e Movimentos Sociais.*

3. *Movimento dos Trabalhadores Rurais sem Terra.*

4. This expression is usually employed to refer to the earlier hostile criticism of the neoliberal economic system by anti-globalization militants (particularly involving the extreme left), including the occurrence of incidences of violence resulting in human injuries (at times even casualties) and damage to private and public properties.

5. The WSF Internet site furnished a complete physical address of this office, plus the relevant telephone and fax numbers (i.e., WSF http://www.forumsocial mundial.org.br; accessed March 15, 2010). There was however a discernable absence of an email address, a highly uncommon practice among contemporary global social networks and movements. This was certainly due to the concern of having to respond to numerous email queries coming from different parts of the world. This seems to indicate that this central body possessed a relatively small and insufficient administrative and public relations capacity.

6. *Associação Brasileira de Organizações Não Governamentais.*

7. *Rede Social de Justiça e Direitos Humanos.*

8. *Comissão Brasileira de Justiça e Paz.*

9. *Instituto Brasileiro de Análises Sociais e Econômicas.*

10. WSF. http://www.forumsocialmundial.org.br/main.php?id_menu=4_2_2_1 &cd_languages=2 (accessed January 10, 2010).

11. WSF. http://www.forumsocialmundial.org.br/dinamic.php?pagina=ci_regras_miami_ing (accessed January 10, 2010).

12. This was not any minor issue. For example, the discussion regarding the selection of Mumbai as a location for hosting the 2004 international social forum went on for several months. Moreover, the Indian national team seemingly had

little say in terms of the final decision that was taken, as writes one of the key architects of the Mumbai forum:

"The decision to make the meeting an Asian meeting was also not taken by WSF India but by the IC. The 'expectation' of the Council was then communicated to WSF India, and largely in order to demonstrate a spirit of solidarity of purpose. . . . In many ways, WSF India thereby became the implementing agency" (Sen 2004: 297).

13. WSF. http://www.forumsocialmundial.org.br/download/2009-02-belem_IC_meeting_report_EN_FINAL_DRAFT.pdf (accessed January 10, 2010).

14. The WSF usually sought to provide participants coming from the poorer countries with air transport and subsistence allowances, and there was also the requirement for the organization to have to cover much of the costs relating to the hiring of local administrative staff, meeting spaces and other infrastructures, essential equipments, security and sanitation services and provisioning of translation. Furthermore, it is worth noting that, from the financial point of view, Brazil, as a middle income country, was not particularly a low-cost location for holding of worldwide social forums. Based on the total budget required for holding of the Mumbai 2004 international forum, India, for example, stood to be a considerably inexpensive location.

15. Unless cited, the information on the WSF finance comes from Ghimire 2006: 4–10.

16. See, for example, Bonfond. http://www.forumsocialmundial.org.br/noticias_textos.php?cd_news=357 (accessed January 10, 2010).

5

Organizational and Mobilization Constraints

What were the exact magnitudes of the organizational and mobilizational difficulties that the WSF confronted as a transnational social movement? More significantly, were these complications susceptible to threats to its basic organizational make-up, rationality or wider values? Considering the existence of numerous limitations on organizational and financial matters, one could argue that movement had already reached an apex in terms of its expansion potential, and that the consolidation of its past success was also not completely guaranteed. In an attempt to explaining some of these key critical organizational and mobilizational constraints, in this chapter, we will look more carefully at the dimensions of representation and internal democracy along with the question of financial sustainability. Additionally, we will consider how its new methods of conceiving political mobilization based on a pluralistic intellectual approach were faring in actual reality. The examples we take up for elaboration will include the movement's declared objective of making use of an expanded set of languages and ideas reflecting a wide range of cultural diversity.

REPRESENTATION AND INTERNAL DEMOCRACY

In the previous chapter, we outlined the broad organizational structure of the WSF consisting of a central Secretariat, the Brazilian Organization Committee, national and regional organizing committees and the IC. Undoubtedly, this last organ was the most pivotal constituent in the movement's chain of command. This body, as seen before, was responsible for conceiving the movement's long-term vision, as well as ensuring the successful organization of social forums at the international and regional levels. The IC was created in 2001 with an initial number of 55 members. Since the Brazilian Organizing Committee was the prime stimulus for the creation of the IC, all of its members (totaling eight in 2001) automatically obtained membership, thereby forming the largest single bloc within this body. Another 58 new members were added in 2003, thus bringing the size of the IC to 113 members. Finally, two other groups of 33 and 10 new members were included in 2006 and 2008, respectively. As a result, by early 2008, the total number of organizations representing the IC stood to be 156 (see Table 2).

According to an initial formal text published by the WSF, the constitution of the IC was conditional to its conforming to a geographical and regional balance aimed at maintaining the diversity of representation among social movements and organizations.[1] Table 3 summarizes the breakdown of national, regional and international representation in the IC between 2003 and 2008. In light of this information, it would seem that, among those organizations enjoying a membership of the IC, there was a reasonably well-balanced representation of national, regional and international organizations. However, over the years, the proportion of national and international organizations considerably increased as compared to that of regional organizations. This is because the South American organizations, notably the Brazilian ones, continued to form a principal segment among national organizations, while new members were added from other countries. As for the international organizations, a vast majority of them came from the Northern countries with relatively easy access to public and private funds for travel as well as with an informed organizational leadership eager to attend various social forums and the IC's internal meetings. On the other hand, for most of the representatives of regional organizations especially those coming from Asia and Africa, any important investment in the WSF activities frequently meant an expensive business in terms of their financial and human resources given the need to have to travel intercontinental distances. As a consequence of this situation, their representation at the IC

Table 2.   The Composition of the WSF's International Committee, 2001–2008

Year	Number of social organizations composing the WSF's International Committee
2001	55
2003	113
2006	146
2008	156

Source: Data for 2001: Whitaker 2006: 38; Data for 2003 to 2008 were prepared by the author based on various documents posted on the WSF Internet site: http://www.forumsocialmundial.org.br (accessed March 15, 2010).

Table 3. The Breakdown of the National, Regional and International Representation to the WSF's International Committee, 2003–2008

Year/total number of organizations	National Representation Number % of organizations		Regional representation Number % of organizations		International representation Number % of organizations	
2003/113	38	33.6	41	36.2	34	30.0
2005/130	40	30.7	45	34.6	45	34.6
2006/146	50	34.2	47	32.1	49	33.5
2008/156	57	36.5	48	30.7	51	32.6

Source: Table prepared by the author based on various documents posted on the WSF Internet site: http://www.forumsocialmundial.org.br (accessed March 15, 2010).

proportionately declined percentagewise—from 36.2 percent in 2003 to 30.7 percent in 2008—despite a slight increase in the total number of organizations involved (i.e., from 41 organizations in 2003 to 48 organizations in 2008; see Table 3).

For historic reasons, South America and Europe have plainly dominated the IC, representing 60 percent of its membership in 2008 (see Table 4). Considering that North America procured another 10 percent of the membership meant that Asia, Eastern Europe, Africa and the Near East combined were left with around 30 percent of the IC's membership. The share of the African participation has somewhat increased in recent years (from 7.9 percent in 2003 to 11.5 percent in 2008) due primarily to the dynamism created by the organization of an international social forum in Nairobi in January 2007. On the other hand, despite its huge size, and despite the fact that richer countries from the region such as Australia, New Zealand, Japan and South Korea were included in the figure, the continental representation from Asia was remarkably low, at about 11 percent in 2008. This suggests that stimulus provided by the organization of the global social forum in Mumbai in 2004 was not sufficient to altering the situation in any significant manner. Since most of the global forums were held in Brazil, travel costs proved particularly onerous for Asian delegates. Only a selected number of them with sufficient internal resources or ability to raise external funds could travel. Likewise, the Eastern European and Near East regions were very poorly represented. In 2008, they comprised 2.5 percent and 4.4 percent of the IC's total membership, respectively.

From this information, it is evident that the political influence of the WSF was very thinly spread in much of Africa, Asia, Eastern Europe and the Near East. This is critical as the WSF as a network organization maintained no grassroots bases of its own. Consequently, it faced the risk of confronting a major constraint to engaging in an extensive and sustained political mobilization in these regions. Already many of its political calls

Table 4. Regional Representation of Social Organizations to the WSF's International Committee, 2003–2008

	2003		2005		2006		2008	
	No.	*%*	*No.*	*%*	*No.*	*%*	*No.*	*%*
	of organizations represented		*of organizations represented*		*of organizations represented*		*of organizations represented*	
Europe	31	27.4%	40	30.7%	46	31.5%	48	30.7%
Eastern Europe	1	0.8%	4	3.0%	4	2.7%	4	2.5%
Asia	14	12.3%	13	10.0%	15	10.2%	17	10.9%
Africa	9	7.9%	11	8.4%	14	9.5%	18	11.5%
Near East	4	3.5%	4	3.0%	6	4.1%	7	4.4%
South America	40	35.3%	46	35.3%	46	31.5%	46	29.4%
North America	14	12.3%	12	9.2%	15	10.2%	16	10.2%
Total number and % of organizations composing WSF International Committee	113	100%	130	100%	146	100%	156	100%

Source: Table prepared by the author based on various documents posted on the WSF Internet site: http://www.forumsocialmundial.org.br (accessed March 15, 2010).

and campaigns tended to last not long beyond the effervescence of the organization of a particular international social forum. On the whole, the spirit of mobilization was often limited to making the event successful by ensuring a notable public participation and the international media coverage. The question of how to create durable political dynamics among social movements in different parts of the world or exert influence over public institutions aimed at prompting sustained social change seemed to have generally remained a secondary concern in planning for a given regional or international social forum.

Having said this, there was a widespread agreement among the core leaders concerning the lack of a satisfactory representation from outside of South America and Europe. Whitaker, a key leader since the inception of the WSF, stated that "the composition of the International Council is unbalanced in terms of the presence of different countries and regions." At the same time, he allowed that "this extension cannot however be unlimited. A too significant number of participants would make the holding of the meetings and decision making even more difficult" (Whitaker 2006: 126). He wrote this against the background that the decisions made at the IC were frequently based on the consensus rather than the casting of votes, which generally tended to take a considerable amount of time "owing to the large number of people making the Council and their differing sensibilities" (ibid.). In short, a marked tension existed between the movements' desire to broaden the membership base of the IC for allowing a greater equitable regional representation, on the one hand, and restrict the membership to a fewer number with the intention that the essential decisions could be made speedily, on the other.

A part of this tension emanated from the WSF's Charter of Principles itself. This fundamental text notably specified that no one should have any deliberative power on behalf of the movement (Article 6) and that there should be no attempt to directing or constructing hierarchies within the organization (Article 7). Furthermore, it stipulated that the movement should operate in a diversified and decentralized fashion respecting the philosophical and geographical plurality of its composition (Article 8). Yet the IC symbolized as a strong and discernable organizational set up, with key leaders enjoying a considerable degree of deliberative power. At the same time, the primary condition attached to the formal creation and functioning of the IC was that it completely adhered to the WSF's Charter of Principles. The result of this situation was that the movement's chief executive body, for the question of practicality, perpetually followed an ad hoc procedure in making crucial decisions; and above all, it could not afford to appear as being the organization's central bureaucratic apparatus taking binding decisions for every one within the movement.

This blurry organizational structure and decision-making procedure made internal democracy within the IC remain highly precarious. While the Charter of Principles called for "the practices of real democracy" or "participatory democracy" (Article 10), there was no mechanism for contesting the representation within the IC. The basic sets of democratic rules concerning the methods of designation of candidates, access to responsibility, having a voice on major decisions, and the like, remained completely ill-defined. The heart of the matter in this regard was not so much the question of promulgating an electoral system in *stricto sensu*, but more of who should have had the right to represent and speak for the organization and under what criteria. In other words, where did the political legitimacy come from for exercising important organizational power? More precisely, who actually gave the mandate for a certain number of individuals and organizations to assemble at the IC and take essential decisions?

These questions stand out to be entirely valid given the fact that the WSF asserted itself to be a new and rare form of democracy. As outlined above, its formal objectives were to construct and consolidate a meaningful and comprehensive participatory representative system within the organization. Furthermore, the movement was seeking to demonstrate its relevance to the wider debates of political representation. To be more precise, the movement considered itself to be a "democratic innovation" capable of reducing the existing forms of deficits in global democratization through constructive criticism and example setting (see on this, for example, Teiv-ainen 2002: 621).

ASCENDANCY OF FINANCE

Ever since the setting up of the IC, the issue of finance remained its primary concern. This is because the organization critically needed funds for ensuring its minimum sets of activities. The availability of additional financial resources also meant the possibility of organizing more extensive and increased number of events, thereby also giving leeway to making a certain degree of impact on the media coverage and public policy discussions. The selection of a place to host a major social forum, whether global or regional was entirely based on the availability of funding, or perceived capacity of national or regional organizations to raise additional funds. This partly explained why the IC took several months to decide on the application of the Indian national organization committee seeking to hold the 2004 Mumbai World Social Forum, as has been noted earlier. Similar sorts of circumstances persisted in the case concerning the selection of Nairobi as a potential African venue for holding the 2007 global event; and this was so despite the fact that IC was clearly pressed to display solidarity with the Nairobi organization team. Following the organization of global social forums in Latin America and Asia (e.g., Mumbai), the African continent was the natural candidate in hosting this meeting.[2]

The financial matters received pre-eminence at all of the IC meetings beginning from its first Dakar meeting in November 2001 to Belem meeting in February 2009.[3] As such, it is not surprising that among the IC's six commissions, the Finance Commission acquired a prominent place. Although this Commission did not directly manage the regular day-to-day financial matters of the movement, it was consistently alarmed that the course and extent of the WSF expansion and activities were being negatively affected due to the lack of adequate funding. The data is eloquent regarding these financial difficulties: by 2005, the WSF spent for different events as much as 14.6 million USD.[4] Also by this time, as was mentioned before, the movement incurred a deficit of about 1.5 million US dollar. Five major Brazilian social organizations: the ABONG, Federation of Agencies for Social and Educational Assistance (FASE[5]), IBASE, Institute of Socioeconomic Studies (INESC[6]) and Trade Union of Federal District Teachers (SINPRO[7]) alone advanced some 629,000 USD in order to ensure that the vital WSF activities could take place as planned.[8] However, given the recurrent situation of the WSF budget deficits, these organizations were not timely reimbursed, thereby considerably affecting their own basic activities.

The primary reason for this financial weakness was the absence of a stable internal financial reserve. The basic source of the WSF's internal income was the registration fees that the individual and organizational delegates paid in order to participate in the forum. However, this income usually constituted less than 10 percent of its overall budget. Furthermore, given its open opposition to the liberal market economy and its negative consequences on social and environmental conditions, the WSF could not afford to seek donations from the international financial institutions, transnational companies or rich governments in the North that openly promoted such policies. In the past, the movement was provided with occasional financial supports by the left leaning governments in Europe. Within Brazil, the movement benefited a sizeable financial assistance from the local municipality and provincial states, federal government and public or semi-public financial or business enterprises such as the Brazilian petroleum company (Petrobras) (Diaz 2006: 96). Once more, owing to the fact that the WSF's Charter of Principles viewed any direct links with the political parties and governments undesirable, the movement as a rule was required to be extremely watchful in creating ostensible and lasting ties with political parties, governments, and other public bodies. This situation put the organization in an extremely odd position when seeking financial assistance from these sources.

Details on the incomes and expenditures of the WSF between 2001 and 2005 are provided in Table 5. It may be seen from the information that the international NGOs remained a very important reliable source of the organization's funding, involving a total of 6.3 million USD and covering over 43 percent of its expenses. This was followed by the financing of WSF activities by the different Brazilian sources, which stood to be 5.2 million USD or 35.5 percent of its total budget. Given that the Brazilian national funding tended to be "in resources and in kind,"[9] for its basic expenditures, the movement was required to heavily rely on international NGO donor agencies such as the Oxfam, Ford Foundation and the church-based agencies such as the Humanist Institute for Cooperation with Developing Countries (HIVOS[10]), Inter-church organization for development cooperation (ICCO[11]) and Church Development Service (EED[12]).

Certain observers within the movement, such as Samir Amin, were concerned that these international NGOs, with the virtue of their capacity to provide important financial support wielded enormous power within the IC, thereby preventing any radicalization in the WSF strategies.[13] François Houtard seemed even more explicit on this. He wrote:

The most powerful organizations from a financial point of view have been able to occupy a larger space, which means more activities, than others with

Table 5. Financial Sources of the WSF, 2001–2005 (in US dollar)

International NGOs		
Oxfam Novib		1,999,434
HIVOS		1,020,040
Ford Foundation		1,098,039
ICCO		573,904
EED		441,531
Action Aid		167,003
CCFD		158,445
Christian Aid		133,770
Rockefeller Brothers		50,000
Misereor		31,802
Development and Peace		23,028
Others		625,557
	Sub-total	6,322,553
		(43.1%)
Bilateral agencies		
SIDA		734,788
SDC		69,124
	Sub-total	803,912
		(5.4%)
Brazilian sources		
Local municipality and government		2,164,396
Federal government		1,147,385
Brazilian enterprises		1,896,644
	Sub-total	5,208,425
		(35.5%)
Other		
Registration fees		2,203,957
WSF's own investment and other		96,814
	Sub-total	2,300,771
		(15.7%)
Total		14,635,661

Source: WSF. http://www.wsflibrary.org/index.php/Image:wsf-FinancialstrategyReport.pdf (accessed February 10, 2010).

less means. It is not necessarily a policy of domination, but a social law which indicates that the necessity of certain rules to avoid that the "law of the market" affects also the full liberty of expression, which is central in the definition of the Forums.[14]

Despite this recognition, international NGOs were fundamental to the very survival of the WSF. So were the Labor Party controlled Brazilian municipalities, provincial governments and the federal State. As a matter of fact, within Brazil, the WSF leadership also attempted to attract the attention of the national business community by seeking to substantiate that the holding of the WSF events in the country stood economically gainful to the business sector. According to its estimation, the WSF in Porto Alegre in 2005, for example, generated as much as 60 million USD worth of direct and indirect benefits for the city, provincial State and the country (in the form of purchase of airline tickets, paying of airport taxes, staying in the hotels, eating at restaurants and using of local transports by the forum's participants, notably international delegates).[15]

In a nutshell, the WSF leadership continued to explore a variety of means for strengthening the movement's financial solidity (including those considered in the past to be frequently politically inappropriate, such as the seeking of donations from international business companies). For example, an expert report on financial strategy commissioned by the IC in 2006 recommended soliciting support from the international business groups that adapted the practice of corporate social responsibility, particularly the airline companies and hotel chains. Among other various recommendations prescribed, this report suggested exploring the strategy of creating reliable solidarity funds (i.e., built on the contributions from the sympathizers of the movement), carrying out publicity campaigns in international newspapers for donations, organizing musical concerts, making use of music downloads to raise funds and seeking commissions and gifts from individual and solidarity groups through Internet payments.[16]

These methods of raising funds were not new inventions since large international organizations such as the Red Cross, World Wildlife Fund, as well as much of the United Nations system already utilized many of these strategies. But pursuing these sorts of fund raising measures by a social movement which overtly criticized the structure of the current economic and political system was clearly risky business as this could invite severe criticism internally as well as from its foes. All the same, securing the basic financial needs was already an excessively heavy burden to the organization. Overall, the contradiction between the internal financial requirements and various reformist propositions advanced to raise funds was so enormous that in the end, the movement chose simply to consent to follow the status quo. In any event, on the basis of the information posted on its Internet site, the movement was not engaged in pursuing any of these proposals in a serious manner. This seemed to have been so at least until the first half of 2010.

THE MOVEMENT'S DIFFICULTIES IN TRANSLATING ITS PLURALISTIC APPROACH TO LANGUAGES AND IDEAS

The campaign to construct "another world" based on a wide range of cultural diversity was the essence of the WSF political engagement. The importance of cultural diversity was justified on two grounds. First, the movement was opposed to the "reductionist views of economy, development and history" (Article 10). Here it sought to put accent basically on the continued problem of "euro-centrism" in interpreting human history, development of knowledge and theory of progress (see on this, for example, Hopkins 2002: 11–36; Wallerstein 2006: 51–70). In particular, it argued that the Western European historical experience or "civilization achievement" (including that of North America since the mid 19th century) did not necessarily represent universal values. Accordingly, the rest of the world could not be reduced simply to being as "local," "traditional" or "backward."

Second, the movement believed in "equality" among peoples and ethnicities, thus condemned "all forms of domination and subjection" (Article 10). Indeed, according to Bernard Cassen (thus a leading figure behind the founding of the WSF), the alternative globalization movement, on its totality, could only be "multipolar, multicultural and multilinguist" (Cassen 2003: 31). Nevertheless, how did the WSF apply these various notions in concrete situations? We were interested in looking at the particular dimensions of languages and ideas.

The Dimension of Languages

Regarding the issue of languages, the basic premise of the movement was grounded on the following: since the language was a "social institution" (Rousseau 1781: 6),[17] a given language within a certain historical and social context could well reinforce the structures of domination (Bloch 1975: 7–8). Obviously, the central reference was made here to the overwhelming and continued domination of the English language in international economy, politics, academic research and writings, in particular with the sustenance of the world's leading political power and economy: the United States. As such, the WSF's fundamental idea was to recognize the importance of the multitude of languages other than being limited merely to English. The campaign to a multi-linguistic approach was also founded on the rationale that its own organizational message could be better propagated to wider areas (i.e., particularly to the countries and regions where English or other prime international or colonial languages were not spoken or fully grasped).

The WSF thus made a resolute effort, right from its first international forum in Porto Alegre in January 2001, to use English, French, Portuguese and Spanish as four official languages. In addition to this, at global and regional forums a simultaneous translation was provided in numerous regional and national languages. However, with the growth in the number of people participating in different forums, the multiplicity of languages used and needs for translation increased. Unpaid layperson interpretation helped to meet some of this requirement. However, the bulk of the translation in four main languages was assured by Babel, an international network of translators and a member of the IC since 2004. The costs for translation for Babel's professional translators and hiring of translation materials stood to be very "high" for the movement (Whitaker 2006: 120).[18] Indeed, given this financial burden, the total number of languages being interpreted during the Nairobi world social forum was brought down basically to two principal colonial languages, namely English and French. Furthermore, the quality of translation as well as audio equipments provided remained frequently very poor.[19]

Even in the case of the four principal languages which the WSF was seeking to maintain equilibrium in their use, the dominance of certain languages became increasingly palpable. Table 6 sheds light on this situation. An inventory of articles assessing the outcome of the world social forums between 2001 and 2008 published on the movement's Internet site pointed towards a rapid pre-eminence of the English language. In 2007, the articles published in English comprised 54 percent of the total articles, while this percentage was only 27 percent in 2001.

The French language, too, was able to maintain a certain degree of significance, with an increase of articles in this language from 9 percent in 2001 to over 28 percent in 2007. This was without a doubt due to a continued heavy investment on the movement by the French intellectual circle, as, in general, the French language has experienced a steady decline in its use in international arenas such as the United Nations system (Calvet 2002: 194–195).

The Spanish language, on the other hand, saw a spectacular decline, constituting only about 6 percent of the total articles published in 2007, as compared to about 18 percent in 2001. We have no specific explanation for this. Nevertheless, one possible reason could be that some of the Spanish-language authors simply chose to write their contributions in English for an enhanced international readership and media coverage.

Finally, the influence of the Portuguese language deteriorated quite significantly. Indeed, in 2001 the share of the Portuguese language articles was about 45 percent of the total articles, which dropped to as low as 11 percent in 2007. Given the fact that the majority of the world social summits were held in Brazil (thus a Portuguese-speaking country with an important academic tradition in writing in Portuguese), such a sharp decline was clearly unexpected. Again one speculative explanation to this could be that some of the earlier Portuguese-language authors switched to English. Another explanation could be that the Brazilian intelligence behind the movement was more and more preoccupied with the logistical matters (in order to make the events exultant and successful), thus could not afford to actively

Table 6. The WSF's Ability to Maintain Diversity of Languages and Ideas (Based on the inventory of articles assessing the outcome of the WSF events between 2001 and 2008)

I. Language in which the article was published

Year	English No.	% of articles	Spanish No.	% of articles	French No.	% of articles	Portuguese No.	% of articles	Other No.	% of articles	Total number of articles
2001	3	27.3%	2	18.1%	1	9.0%	5	45.4%	0	0.0%	11
2002	6	15.8%	15	39.5%	6	15.8%	11	28.9%	0	0.0%	38
2003	11	35.5%	6	19.3%	3	9.7%	9	29.0%	2	6.4%	31
2004	21	56.7%	8	21.6%	2	5.4%	4	10.8%	2	5.4%	37
2005	10	34.4%	11	37.9%	3	10.3%	5	17.2%	0	0.0%	29
2006	15	28.3%	19	35.8%	5	9.4%	13	24.5%	1	1.8%	53
2007	19	54.2%	2	5.7%	10	28.5%	4	11.4%	0	0.0%	35
2008	No articles published as there was no formal forum organized in 2008										

II. Regional origin of authors

Year	North America No.	% of authors	South America No.	% of authors	Europe No.	% of authors	Africa & Near east No.	% of authors	Asia No.	% of authors	Non-identified No.	% of authors	Total of articles published
2001	2	18.1	4	36.3	3	27.2	0	0.0	1	9.0	1	9.0	11
2002	6	15.7	14	36.8	12	31.5	2	5.2	2	5.2	2	5.2	38
2003	6	19.3	10	32.2	12	38.7	1	3.2	1	3.2	1	3.2	31
2004	5	13.5	11	29.7	10	27.0	2	5.4	9	24.3	0	0.0	37
2005	3	10.3	12	41.3	9	31.0	2	6.8	2	6.8	1	3.4	29
2006	5	9.4	22	41.5	13	24.5	3	5.6	5	9.4	5	9.4	53
2007	5	14.2	8	22.8	12	34.2	5	14.2	3	8.5	2	5.7	35
2008	No articles published as there was no formal forum organized in 2008												

Note: (1) When an article is written by more than one author, only the first author is included in calculation; (2) An author may be an individual or institution; and (3) When the same article is printed in multiple languages, the original language in which the article was written is considered.

Sources: Table prepared by the author based on WSF. "World Social Forum Memorial," "http://www.forumsocialmundial.org.br/main.php?id_menu=14_3&cd_language=2 (accessed January 10, 2010).

take part in intellectual debates and writings. Further research would be needed to substantiate these various points.

THE DIMENSION OF IDEAS

Here the movement's central argument was that a greater diversity of thoughts, expressed in part in local languages and other cultural attributes (arts, literature, way of life, value systems and traditions), should be promoted on their own merit. It held in particular that there was nothing like a "superior idea" as frequently implied in the Eurocentric outlook. Therefore, the intent of organizing the world social forums was basically to provide an outlet to the diverse ideas emerging from the non-Northern intellectual traditions. While this certainly seemed like sensible thinking, the actual results in this regard, too, were mixed, if not globally disappointing.

Again, as summarized in Table 6, if we consider the regional origin of the authors publishing the lead articles on the result of the world social forums between 2001 and 2008, the authors originating from the European and American regions constituted the largest group, with the authors from European origin increasing their share of articles from 27 percent in 2001 to 34 percent in 2007. On the other hand, the percentage of articles published by North America origin–scholars decreased from 18 to 14 percent (despite an overall growth in the total number of articles published by them, that is, from two articles in 2001 to five articles in 2007). In 2007, the South American and Africa/Near-east origin authors made up of 8 and 14 percent of the authors, respectively. One can discern that the representation of authors from the Asian continent was particularly low, about 8.5 percent in 2007; and this has not altered since 2001. We believe the explanation was to be found partly in the long and expensive travel distance to Brazil where the majority of the global forums were held. The inability to participate in these meetings obviously meant a lack of ability to fully observe and grasp the debates that took place, hence the difficulty in writing any perceptible or timely articles.

While the cultural diversity based on multiple languages and thoughts continued to stand as the WSF's declared philosophical principle and while an attempt was also made to translating its pluralistic approach to languages and ideas, in practice the movement managed to produce few tangible results. Overall, the apparent European or Western domination in terms of both the use of languages and the basic source of ideas fed into the WSF process could not be changed. Thus, despite having identified the core problematic and having introduced a certain number of novel measures, the movement was unable to integrate a pluralistic intellectual approach even within its internal functioning. Changing this externally was obviously even more complicated.

NOTES

1. WSF. http://www.forumsocialmundial.org.br/main.php ?id_menu=4_2_2_1 &cd_language=2 (accessed January 10, 2010).

2. In the case of the Nairobi world social forum, besides the financial issue, many powerful Brazilian organizations behind the WSF movement were increasingly concerned that this emblematic event could gradually be going away from Brazil. Given their historic leadership role, they strongly desired that the key international event continued to stay in the country.

3. WSF. http://www.forumsocialmundial.org.br/main.php?id_menu=3_2_2&cd_language=2 (accessed February 10, 2010).

4. WSF. http://www.wsflibrary.org/index.php/image:wsf-financialstrategyreport.pdf; p. 12 (accessed February 10, 2010).

5. *Federação de Órgãos Para Assistência Social e Educacional.*

6. *Instituto de Estudios Socioeconómicos.*

7. *Sindicato dos Professores do Distrito Federal.*

8. WSF. http://www.forumsocialmundial.org.br/download/carta_doacoes_FSM_por.pdf; p. 8 (accessed February 10, 2010).

9. WSF. http://www.wsflibrary.org/index.php/image:wsf-financialstrategyreport.pdf; p. 31 (accessed February 10, 2010).

10. *Humanistisch Instituut voor Ontwikkelingssamenwerking.*

11. *Interkerkelijke Organisatie voor Ontwikkelingssamenwerking.*

12. *Evangelische Entwicklungs Dienst.*

13. Amin, Samir. "Le Forum Social Mondial est-il utile pour les luttes populaires ?" WSF. http://www.forumsocialmundial.org.br/noticias_textos.php?cd_news=349 (accessed February 10, 2010).

14. Houtard, François. "The world social forum in Nairobi," http://www.forumsocialmundial.org.br/noticias_textos.php?cd_news=354 (accessed February 10, 2010).

15. WSF. http://www.forumsocialmundial.org.br/download/carta_doacoes_FSM_por.pdf; p. 3 (accessed February 10, 2010).

16. WSF. http://www.wsflibrary.org/index.php/image:wsf-financialstrategyreport.pdf; pp. 33–36 (accessed February 10, 2010).

17. Rousseau. http://classiques.uqac.ca/classiques/Rousseau_jj/essai_origine_des_langues/origine_des_langues.pdf (accessed February 10, 2010). Indeed, Rousseau considered the language to be "the first social institution."

18. A report of the delegates from the WSF India also suggested that the costs for the translation at the WSF 2003 (including the travel expenses for translators) were around 300,000 USD. WSF India. "Report of the meeting of the International Council, Miami, USA, June 23–26, 2003" (unpublished).

19. As a matter of fact, this was also the case with the Mumbai world social forum held in 2004 (personal observation).

IV

SYNTHESES AND CONCLUSIONS

6

Mechanisms and Exercise of Power

In the preceding chapters, we reviewed the structure and modus operandi of interactions between international and national actors with particular reference to the four single-issue-oriented transnational campaigns and the WSF. With regard to the former movements, international actors seemed to exercise a considerable degree of influence over their national counterparts. Indeed, having to critically rely on external financing and ideas, the national groups found themselves largely in a subordinated position, often merely executing the calls and instructions coming from the international level.

As to the WSF, despite numerous organizational and mobilization constraints, the IC continued to function as a supreme body deciding on all crucial strategic matters concerning the movement's philosophical values, its future direction, all matters relating to the holding of regional and global forums, as well as the question of national and regional representation. The WSF as an international social movement sought to justify its distinctiveness on the basic line of reasoning that its internal functioning and construction of external coalitions were governed by true democratic spirit. In other words, from the top to the bottom of the organization, all individuals and groups engaged within the movement were seen as being fundamentally equal. In particular, no dictate or manipulation of power should occur inside the movement. For example, its Charter of Principles formally rejected the idea of taking decisions as a collective body so as to prevent that movement becoming "a locus of power" (Article 6: see Figure 3), or "a new space of fight for hegemony or power thereby dividing its participants and weakening the movement," according to one of its founding leaders (Whitaker 2006: 17).

Even in the case of the transnational campaigns on debt relief, trade justice, corruption control and currency transactions taxation, the essence of their message remained quite comparable to that of the WSF. These movements considered themselves to be the result of an extensive and worldwide representation of NGOs and numerous other types of social movements; they purposefully worked towards strengthening the Southern voice; and they functioned as a collective platform of diverse groups of social forces and organizations aimed at facilitating a wide exchange of ideas and information in their area of specialization.

How should one comprehend then this inbuilt paradox between the stated egalitarian conception of the movement, on the one hand, and the incidence of internal power concentration in the hands of international actors, on the other? Perhaps one way to explain is to say that declarations were basic organizational intents. Accordingly, there was no guarantee as such that these objectives or targets were to be implemented in actual reality, given especially the innumerable difficulties that these social movements frequently faced. Another way to explain is to point out that fine declarations and expressions of intentions were clearly indispensable, if the organization were to attract resources and potential supporters or allies. Moreover, continued strategic announcements were fundamental to retain those who had already chosen to join the organization.

Nevertheless, following the formulation of a grand vision, a logical path for these movements was evidently to seek to put them into a tangible operation. We believe it was at the level of the implementation that power relations tended to particularly manifest. We may recall that the declarations on the founding of four transnational campaigns as well as the WSF could take place at the international level without any difficulties. Serious complications steadily began to surface when these initiatives needed to be operationalized at the country level with the formation of national collaborating teams or establishment of cooperative links with wider circles of like-minded individuals and groups. It was from this moment precisely that international actors were required to delicately use their influence, appearing on the surface to be open-minded and equal to their collaborators, while in reality constantly seeking to maintain an overall command over the core organizational activities and strategic directions. Meanwhile, the requirement to have to establish relationships with national level social actors combined with a skillful and circumspect use of influence was that various distinctive and adept forms of organizational hierarchy, legitimacy attainment, zones of uncertainty and representation systems had to be invented, preserved and constantly adjusted. In elaborating and implementing specific localized program activities or international campaigns at different stages of the organizational evolution, the movements' internal structures as well as their external interactions were therefore required to incorporate numerous obscurities and tensions.

INFORMAL HIERARCHY

From the onset, both the selected four transnational campaigns and the WSF emphasized the significance of informal hierarchical arrangements. Evidently, conceiving of a hierarchy with a chain of command from the superior to the subordinates did not correspond to their fundamental organizational values which frequently called for increased "democracy," "justice," "equality" and "solidarity" at various levels. In any event, most of these movements retained no reliable or sufficient resources to create a costly formal bureaucratic structure, with sizeable staff, office equipments, or administrative edifices (for headquarters as well as national and regional branches). Furthermore, since the bulk of the mobilizing efforts of the selected transnational campaigns as well as the WSF were limited to short time intervention cycles or specific activities such as the lobbying, holding of meetings and organizing of public demonstrations at international events (notably international conferences, and regional and global forums in the case of the WSF) as mentioned before, there was little need to maintain a permanent and full-size administration. The central administration in actual fact could remain very slim, even inactive for much of the year, as long as it could be promptly reactivated to handle the basic organizational activities.

Despite a svelte management, the results of this study showed that, each of these two categories of movements was clearly comprised of a central authority with leaders, ideologues or experts. These individuals performed multi-fold jobs animating militants and supporters internally and developing collaborative links with external groups, the media and public authority.

At the same time, many of these individuals, albeit evidently extremely powerful within their respective organizations were not always able to openly claim authority. At times they were constricted to remain in the backseat or even in obscurity. The reason for this was simple: there was a constant requirement to demonstrate the existence of a "flat" hierarchy within the movement, and in particular to signify that the movement functioned within the principles of equality of responsibility and leadership-sharing vis-à-vis the Southern leaders or national and regional representative organizations. This feature was observable nearly in all of the transnational campaigns covered in the study, including a relatively structured anti-corruption campaign. For example, each year when the TI released its annual corruption indices report ranking countries in accordance to their success in implementing the overall corruption control targets, it was rather the organization that was brought into the limelight rather than its director or senior cadres; this was obviously meant to display that the report was the result of a collective work brining together numerous experts, human rights organizations and national teams. Likewise, in the case of the transnational campaigns relating to debt relief, trade justice and international transaction taxation proposition, no top figures could surface straightforwardly. The Internet websites of these movements frequently avoided publicizing the profile and stature of their principal leaders.

With respect to the WSF, manifestly, a number of personalities have continued to make known their presence ever since the holding of its first global social forum in Porto Alegre in January 2001. Francisco Whitaker, Oded Grajew and Bernard Cassen have been considered to be the original initiators of the movement. However, they have not sought to occupy any open frontline responsibility in recent years. Candido Grzybowski has probably been the prime figure in recent years, negotiating funds with the Brazilian government and directing much of the functioning of the IC. Yet apart from the occasional interviews in the media during the time of the global forums, this personage has tended to present himself as a simple director of a Brazilian national think-tank research institute (cf. IBASE) in Rio de Janeiro.[1] Samir Amin and Walden Bellow, representing respectively Africa and Asia, have been two other historic celebrities; and a number of academics, NGOs, foundations and trade union figures from Western Europe, Scandinavia and North America have also comprised a significant proportion of the WSF's leadership.[2] These different personalities have acted upon as primary leaders and strategists, mobilizing resources critical to the dynamics of the movement as well as enjoying considerable support from the individual followers and participant organizations. In any event, nearly all of these leaders have been represented at the IC thanks to the membership of their own organizations in this influential body.

Is this informal hierarchy more suited to establishing an equitable and long-term relationship with national actors, rather than if it were of a formal nature? We have no comparative information on this, but the guess is that, despite an unstructured organizational configuration and general democratic spirit with many influential leaders seemingly agreeing to remain on the backseat, in seeking vital information and resources, national actors were nevertheless required to pass through these select few. Similarly, the key leaders carried on giving interviews to the press, wrote in specialized journals and participated in international conferences speaking favorably to their campaigns or movements. Overall, they sought to demonstrate that they were indispensable on tactical and theoretical matters, as well as in extending an enhanced public image of the organization. Consequently, they remained in a good position to maintain sway over the prime strategy and activities of their movements, albeit renouncing the formal day-to-day managerial activities in certain cases.

GAINING OF LEGITIMACY THROUGH MIXED RESOURCES

This brings us to the question of legitimacy. In other words, how did leaders and transnational movements manage to justify their commanding positions? We believe that one prime source of this power was geography. Among the four international campaigns, three held headquarters in the North; and within the debt movement, although one powerful constituent (i.e., the Jubilee South) maintained a formal head office in Manila, nearly all of its potent leaders and networks were based in the United Kingdom, Belgium or Germany. Concerning the WSF, it should be recalled that the movement was originally conceived in Geneva and its European and American affiliates ever since its inception have continued to play a leading role within the movement. This is in some ways quite understandable since it is in Europe or North America that the headquarters of most of the key protagonist international organizations are to be found: International Monetary Fund, World Bank, World Trade Organization, G8 (now G20), United Nations, European Union, etc. Furthermore, it is in these two regions that the majority of the world conferences have taken place. Therefore the ability to mount contestations in these parts of the world tended to give visibility to the movements' themes, including a certain degree of hope for policy changes by the powerful international organizations or Northern governments. Accordingly, specialists on transnational social movements such as Sydney Tarrow have stated these settings to be extremely important for accessing political opportunities and resources crucial for international militancy (Tarrow 2005: 6–10). Obviously, the existence of such opportunities and resources in particular geographical locations also meant that certain key individuals and social movements coming from these regions were particularly well placed in rationalizing and strengthening their position.

The second source of legitimacy was history. Since the 18th century, Europe, followed then by North America, has functioned as the world center for knowledge not only in natural sciences and their application, but also in all of social sciences, including the invention of major political ideologies. As such, the leaders and movements emanating from these regions held a privileged position to construct relevant discourses. They were particularly at ease in the crafting and packaging of many noble ideas as well as institutionalizing them in the form of global campaigns and movements. Naturally, one could also see the presence of a certain number of privileged intellectuals from the Southern regions in this process.[3] Nevertheless, they,

too, were usually taught in Western universities or curricula. Rather predictably, Europe continued to serve as a prime focus of their historical and
ideological references.

Of course, many of these leaders did recognize that there was an endur-
ing problem of modeling the whole world according to the experience of
European history. Indeed, in the case of the WSF, in specific, a deliberate
attempt was made to conceive a political project based on a greater degree
of cultural representation expressed in the plurality of ideas and languages.
Yet the actual results in this regard remained rather disappointing, as previously observed. Having said this, in general terms, the leaders of the WSF
as well as other transnational campaigns included in the study were clearly
adept in constructing new and sufficiently attractive discourses that helped
justify their overall importance. From this standpoint, precisely, Foucault
insisted that "it is in discourse that power and knowledge are joined together" (Foucault 2005: 90).

Additionally, by virtue of being located at the historical and current
center of power, the transnational movements and their leaders were in
a position to get connected and maintain the relationship with diverse
groups of people and social movements worldwide. This wider link with
an important number of social networks, both in the North as in the South,
gave them an additional means of legitimacy (because this corroborated
that they possessed the broad capacity to craft social movements of truly a
global nature). Such prospects, in contrast, were rarely accessible to their
Southern collaborators. As a matter of fact, Southern organizations desiring
to join similar movements in other regions in Asia, Africa or Latin America
were frequently obliged to pass through Northern social networks. In this,
language was one major barrier. Equally significant was the absence of
previous contacts or lack of ability to foster such contacts in a sustained
manner. In light of this, conceiving and animating a worldwide movement
linking diverse social groups, networks and regions from peripheral zones
was a highly difficult task, if not plainly impossible.

Another element of legitimacy was the media connections. This is simply
because the North has remained the world's media hub. Increasingly, however, the use of media (printed as well as audiovisual) has been a question
of individual contacts and the social organization's ability to produce suit-
able professional news items and timely analysis (including the competent
use of international languages). Furthermore, more and more the media
has become not only the prime medium of communication used by transnational contestation organizations and their leaders seeking to influence
the public at large and government institutions, but also to galvanizes its
lower constituents as well as collaborating groups and networks. For this
reason, mastering the flow of information through the media on their

program contents, timetable, the use of eminent personalities and specialists to endorse the movement's strategies and action plans, etc., was utterly important (for a general discussion on this dimension from the point of organization theory see, for example, Hatch and Cunliff 2009: 320). This was particularly so given the fact that the transnational mobilization has now become very much of an affair of international networking and communication, away from the traditional forms of mobilization based typically on a structured organization, membership and group representation.

Finally, besides the intellectual capital and useful relations with the media, a significant degree of legitimacy was gained through the disbursement of funds. Albeit not generating financial resources of their own, transnational social organizations were able to secure sufficient external funds for their minimum operation as well as at times providing financial support to collaborating networks from developing countries. The empirical evidence presented earlier suggested that most national units or collaborating organizations were regularly provided with financial assistance to develop and implement their initial programs in line with international frameworks or planned activities. They also continued to receive a limited amount of funds to cover the costs of their occasional international travel during the subsequent periods.

Handel asserts that an organization's financial resources vulnerability emanates from two dimensions: the criticality of the resources and the relative magnitude of the exchange (Handel 2003: 236). It is not possible to say precisely how much of the national organization's total budget was met by international sources. As for the issue of the financial criticality, it is evident that for most national units or organizations international resources represented the primary, however minimum, sources of finance, thus ensuring their initial program development and continued basic functioning. Although, as was shown in the earlier analysis, this situation induced vulnerability and dependence to national organizations, since the transnational movements were able to mount many fitting program activities that would attract external funding, with some of it going down as material rewards for team working, the coalition organizations at lower levels could not afford to ignore the significance of this collaboration. In some cases, the leading transnational social organizations behind a given campaign retained substantial resources by themselves. This was, for example, the case with Oxfam. Indeed, this organization not only financed the WSF but also several of the transnational campaigns, notably trade justice and debt relief campaigns. Furthermore, national teams frequently received useful counsels and technical assistance from their international counterpart organizations in their own attempt to identify and approach potential funding sources in developed countries.

UNCERTAINTY AN IMPORTANT ASSET

Various scholars within the general corpus of organization theory view uncertainty as a critical problem that managers or leaders must deal with if they wish to successfully exercise authority over their organization. To Pfeffer, for example, certain individuals and departments within the organization ensure their privileged position by virtue of being able to resolve critical problems or obtaining scarce resources (Pfeffer 1981: 110). Likewise, Crozier earlier in his research found out that the ability to deal with uncertainty within the chain of production provided the key individuals, from managers to technicians, with a considerable degree of influence (Crozier 1963: 176–214). In the case of transnational network politics, on the contrary, uncertainty was an inherent mechanism in the production and subtle exercise of power. In this sense, uncertainty stood out to be an asset rather than a liability. Moreover, uncertainty stood to be specifically advantageous to the highest echelon at the international level.

Uncertainty was an integral part of the organizational life of most transnational campaigns and movements. Indeed, uncertainty existed right from their inception. Their generalized aversion to institutionalization or bureaucratization with a structured organizational set up and visible internal hierarchy was that they were necessarily required to choose an informal system of administrative or networking arrangements. In some cases, it was even difficult to say when, how and by whose initiative a specific transnational campaign or social organization had actually come into being. In the specific case of the WSF, for example, one was not entirely sure about the number of people that could be considered as its founding "fathers" and whether it was basically a Brazilian initiative.[4] This situation was not very different with regard to the selected four international campaigns, too. For example, it would be greatly risky to say when the campaigns related to debt relief or trade justice actually started. By and large, the very survival of these and many other similar initiatives as transnational movements was never completely certain.

Regarding the line of ideology chosen, even though these various campaigns and movements commonly criticized the global economic system and prevailing forms of inequalities, as well as called for a greater solidarity among rich and poor nations and people, their formal declarations and the implementation of prime activities at various levels often nurtured ambiguity in their content and course of action so as to attract a maximum number of politically and geographically diverse groups of individuals and social organizations. In other words, espousing uncertainty was more suited in these circumstances than seeking to unravel it. In short, it was extremely problematic to ascertain how different coalitions or social organizations came into existence and what made them in actual fact cooperate with each other. Furthermore, these various transnational social movements eternally harbored uncertainty in dealing with the formal authorities, in particular around the question or the extent to which they should work within the existing institutional parameters.

Uncertainty and indecisiveness were particularly characteristic during the operation phase. In general, no clear rules existed in terms of who was supposed to do what and also what specific activities were to occur at what level (i.e., international, regional or national), including the question of how the central coordination should take place. In particular, the enumeration of organizational work programs consisting of detailed activities, time tables and targets was frequently few and far between. Consequently, it was not so surprising that much of the mobilization and implementation work took place in a highly hotchpotch and unplanned manner.

Finance was another area illustrative of many of these uncertainty conditions. It was obvious that as network organizations with no regular membership base (thus with no guarantee of any constant financial contributions), external financial resources were especially critical for the survival of these social organizations. Yet most of them, as noted beforehand, scarcely received sufficient outside funds which would have eventually helped them to avoid the acute financial uncertainty that they regularly confronted. What were then the most reliable sources for generating external funds and what were the usual conditions attached to them? Under what criteria the allocation of the available resources for different activities, including their use by national units, should take place?

Significantly, who should be responsible for making these crucial decisions? Not least, how should the organization's budget be prepared, how would the accounting be kept and how would they be verified by independent external professional experts? What were the long-term strategies, if any, for handling the organization's current as well impending financial difficulties? The information and debates remained few and blurry on many these essential aspects. In any event, whether the principal organizations or their leaders sufficiently invested in radically altering their overall financial structure or the existing funding system was far from clear. Quite the opposite, uncertain and informal financial arrangements were quite frequently and agreeably suited to fulfill various individual and organizational interests.

Finally, an uncertain and informal functioning meant any critical internal or external assessment of the organization's ongoing activities, overall performance or the effects of certain initiatives undertaken could auspiciously be avoided. There was also little need to have to respond to any intricate questioning on the organization's long term objectives, preferred priority areas or future opportunities and challenges. At the least, this helped central leadership to avoid external budgetary supervision or discussions on new organizational orientations or activities, including any potential resources claims by regional and national teams or other collaborating organizations.

Admittedly, for many, these social organizations, there could be certain judicious reasons for preferring to remain informal or obscure. For example, this could allow them a greater degree of maneuverability in terms of adapting to a rapidly changing situation, deciding upon the choice of alliances to be developed and spontaneous activities to be mounted. Besides, scarce financial and human resources could be deployed swiftly. Nevertheless, it should also be noted that, in both circumstances, i.e., the maintenance of uncertainty in a calculated or earnest manner, the end results were the same: most available financial resources tended to remain in the hands of the central authority.

EXPEDIENCY OF AN OPAQUE REPRESENTATIVE STRUCTURE

The existence of informal hierarchy, concentration of much of the organizational resources in the hands of the few and persistent uncertainty, as observed above, could tell us already a great deal about the nature of the representation system that was actually conceived and put into operation. In general, this system lacked transparency, competence and efficacy. With regard to the WSF's representative structure, we learnt that its central secretariat was barely operational, and that the organization's principal Internet site was generally dormant for much of the year with the exception of the period when the major international forum took place. Most of the WSF's national and regional committees held no offices or clearly designated people to carry out organizational responsibilities. The prime organizational body responsible for strategic as well as operational matters was obviously the IC. As was noted earlier in 2008, this body was composed of some 156 members. Yet on the basis of the information available, it was difficult to discern how these members were selected, including the criteria for their renewal, the procedures and timing of elections of new members, etc. By the same token, it was difficult to know what went on inside the IC. In other words, it was problematic to gauge how certain propositions emerged, who had actually advanced them, for what specific reasons, what was finally decided, and in particular how were different balancing acts carried out?

With regard to the single cause-oriented transnational campaigns, the representative system was just as obscure, if not more. No doubt, in addition to the NGOs and some social organizations that they were able to mobilize, they could claim to have enjoyed a widespread support of the common people, media and public personalities. Nevertheless, each of these campaigns relied essentially on a close circle of individuals and collaborating groups. Even here much of the alliance occurred on an ad-hoc basis, built usually on previous acquaintances. By their very nature, these informal alliances specified no comprehensive goals; nor did they fix any time tables. Leaders and key supporters communicated frequently through the media. In the absence of internal elections or clearly defined organizational sanctions from the constituent groups, they were confined to no specific terms of office or management liability. Similarly, the information concerning the sources and use of resources they mobilized was far from legible.

We may lament this "closed" system and impromptu way of functioning. But such an informal system and obscurity has become nearly an obligatory feature of the transnational network politics. To remedy this, the social organizations would have needed to retain office buildings, a certain number of permanent staff and a reliable financial income. Moreover, a certain form of electoral arrangement and organizational hierarchy would have been necessary. Taken as a whole, this would have made them resemble more comparably the traditional structured movements like the trade unions or political parties. Evidently, this was not the general spirit of the alternative globalization movement, as it looked for fostering popular mobilizations on a voluntary provisioning of time, resources and the display of a certain form of moral conviction that things ought to change. Above and beyond, political systems based on political parties, parliaments and offices were considered to be "distant, undemocratic and non-transparent . . . with increasing bureaucratization of politics itself" (Grzybowski 2003: 10). As such, new innovations that included mobilizations of diverse social groups and organizations around the principles of "non-directivity," "horizontality," "democracy," "diversity," etc., were seen fundamental (Whitaker 2006: 124–126). All told, there was thus the incongruous phenomenon of *arroseur arrosé:*[5] in other words, those claiming that their opponents were not democratic were finding themselves adopting a system that ostensibly lacked an internal democratic representation practice, as well as open and functional management.

At the same time, this opaque nature of functioning and the absence of an internal electoral system produced an atypical form of running and exercising of power within the organization. Michels analyzing the composition and evolution of the leadership within political parties and trade union movements in Europe in the early 20th century suggested that an increase in the organizational complexity, including the technical specialization, made it necessary to call for the intervention of the directing elites. As a result, he argued:

> The power of determination comes to be considered one of the specific attributes of leadership, and is gradually withdrawn from the masses to be concentrated in the hands of the leaders alone. (Michels 1959: 31)

A comparable situation could be observed within the WSF and single-cause transnational movements. They were constantly confronted by having to sharpen campaign themes, look for well-known personalities who could endorse their ideas, identify like-minded groups for potential alliances, solicit increased media coverage, publish and disseminate campaign ideas targeting specific audience groups, raise funds, and so forth. Evidently those who handled these issues satisfactorily could hope to derive swift and considerable organizational resources and authority, including the mandate to take important resolutions and use or withhold information, contacts, knowledge and financial resources under their control for strengthening their own position and line of thinking.

However, unlike Michels who believed that the concentration of power at the top went hand in hand with formalization and bureaucratization of the organization (Michels ibid. 33), within these selected transnational movements, the preservation of power and authority in a small group of leaders was possible by virtue of maintaining an informal and opaque organizational structure. The advantage of this particular modus operandi was that leaders could remain discreet on the procedure and content of key organizational decisions. In particular, they retained considerable capacity to dissimulate compromising information, such as the arrival of funds from certain governments or enterprises with bad environmental and human rights records. Most of all, they could protect themselves from unwarranted questioning by the wider public and media on their working methods and the overall effectiveness of the movement. In addition to this, they were able to avoid leadership competition coming potentially from individuals or groups outside the select inner circle, as well as choose when to remain behind the scenes or come out in the limelight depending upon the specific circumstances.

From the preceding discussion it is evident that, both the selected four transnational campaigns and the WSF presented several innovative organizational qualities. Namely, an informal way of working was the general spirit of these organizations. At the same time, a hierarchy structure began to steadily surface and ultimately became a permanent organizational feature. In the same way, the legitimacy which the leaders enjoyed was not always based on their managerial or leadership competence; nor was this based on their faculty to produce concrete results or overall organizational efficacy. This was built rather on their ability to mobilize mixed resources: their discursive capacity, access to financial resources and geographical and historical power. Likewise, uncertainty appeared to be an important asset for the leadership in their attempt to exercise authority. Finally, the representation system did not stand as "open" or "democratic" as the key leaders and organizational public relations material seemed to imply; on the contrary, a greatly opaque system of operation had been institutionalized, including certain tendencies towards "oligarchy" (to borrow the term from Michels 1959: 32). An overall outcome of these evolutions was that both groups of movements were compelled to internalize a considerable degree of ambiguity in their governing structure and functioning. In actual fact, important organizational adjustments and maneuvering were frequently needed simply to obfuscate this ambiguity.

After having examined the mechanisms and exercise of power inherent in the organizational structures and functioning of its two essential constituents: transnational campaigns and the WSF, in the following chapter, the alternative globalization movement will be analyzed as a single unit.

NOTES

1. It should be noted though that the IBASE is a member of the WSF's Brazilian Organizing Committee as well as the powerful IC.

2. Overall, according to Albert, in 2003, the WSF leadership was composed of "roughly 100 people," Albert. http://www.countercurrents.org/wsf-albert2403.html (accessed April 18, 2010).

3. Some authors have noted that even within this group of Southern leaders, "light-skinned people of European origin" tended to dominate. Here the reference is made in specific to the Brazilian leaders of the WSF (Teivainen 2004: 127).

4. According to certain authors, the "first formulation of the idea is generally attributed to Oded, Grajew" (Teivainen 2004: 122). Others cite Bernard Cassen, then president of ATTAC as being the "spiritual father of the initiative" (Agrikoliansky and Sommier 2005:21). On the other hand, Whitaker, who is regarded as one of the founding personalities of the WSF, on his part, simply acknowledges the movement as a "club" established by "a very close number of deciders" (Whitaker 2006: 129).

5. The waterer watered.

7

Conclusions

Holding of Power by Another Name

The principal task of this work has been to comprehend the organizational configuration and inner functioning of a rather emblematical and considerably acclaimed transnational social organization: the alternative globalization movement. The inquiry was in part guided by the consideration that the existing body of knowledge within the "organization theory" remained fairly limited in the area of nonindustrial, informal and continuously evolving types of social organizations functioning at the global level. The study showed that the mobilization capacity and organizational structure of the alternative globalization movement stretched from the transnational to national levels, as well as industrialized to developing societies. If this organizational dimension and range of activities undertaken are taken into account, the size of operation of the movement would certainly appear to be fairly comparable to an average multinational corporation, for example. In any event, globalization processes have created as much scope for economic enterprises as for citizens, social groups and organizations to promote their claims and create wider coalitions, however unstructured and varied they may be. Above and beyond, the alternative globalization movement gave evidence to a distinct organizational design and discourse deserving a thorough investigation.

Such a distinct feature was precisely the movement's critique to power. Namely, in seeking to meaningfully alter the current economic systems and broader forms of global power relations, it upheld that new forms of inclusive political philosophy and informal representation systems were absolutely vital. As such, it discarded formal, regimented types of organizational construction and working, frequently inherent, for example, in political parties and trade unions, in favor of non-hierarchical and diffused power-sharing practices. The preceding sections described and carefully examined many these aspects. Overall, the research results demonstrated that there was a vast gap between the formally stipulated organizational interpretation of power and the end results that ensued. There were numerous methods and intentions of exercising organizational authority; and nearly like in political parties and trade unions, there was a tendency to power concentration towards the uppermost echelon, and worse yet, the movement embraced significantly a greater degree of organizational obscurity than these traditional forms of political organizations.

By way of conclusion, in this chapter, we would like to emphasize the following three dimensions: (a) an informal organizational structure does not mean that there is an absence of power; (b) the exercise of power takes place while denying it; and (c) there is seemingly a lack of internal resistance to power concentration. In the final section, a critical assessment on the evolving trends in the movement's internal life and power relations will be considered, including the theoretical and empirical implications that arise.

AN INFORMAL ORGANIZATIONAL STRUCTURE DOES NOT MEAN THERE IS ABSENCE OF POWER

An informal organizational structure has been the essence of the alternative globalization movement. The organization advocated internal democracy and equality of treatment among all participating groups and organizations. In particular, it was implied that a high level of organizational formalization would entail maintaining of headquarters and branches, directors, commissions, senior cadres, as well as employees, thus potentially producing many unintended consequences like the creation of a visible and burdensome internal organizational hierarchy with an upward centralization of authority. In effect, as we observed above, the internal hierarchy and concentration of power were not altogether missing. The point that should therefore be underlined here is that merely stating an informal and non-hierarchical organizational structure as being the guiding principles or methods of operation did not mean that there was in reality a complete absence of power. In this respect, we believe two points deserve particular attention.

First, the key decision-making power and other organizational resources were clearly located at the top of the hierarchy. With regard to the WSF, the IC, the peak of the pyramid, held these vital resources. The same was true concerning the four transnational campaigns, as it was essentially their international headquarters that accrued most organizational resources. Whether it was the WSF or four transnational movements, aside from the elaboration of the essential political strategy and parameters of actions, it was at the summit that much of the crucial organizational strategy and programs, including the choice of different agenda or action plans, was developed. It was also at this level that decisions pertaining to the extension of the movement to specific countries or regions or creating of tactical alliances with certain actors, including public institutions, took place. Additionally, it was here that the bulk of fund-raising activities involving both private and public sources were organized, while lower levels were frequently reduced to obtaining endorsements and recommendations from the center. More significantly, the flow of primary decisions and fundamental resources always tended to flow from above to below, and seldom from below to above.

Second, the evidence that emerged most clearly from the previous discussion was the trend towards the exercise of a considerable degree of organizational power by a few privileged individuals. The prime responsibilities of these select few included the working out of the movement's strategic ideological orientation as well as ensuring its continued application, setting up of crucial rules and procedures, deciding on the issue for external alliances and cooperation, formulating of advocacy or campaign agendas, organizing of specific events, and so forth. These leaders were not exactly the same type as former political party or trade union chiefs typically maintaining relatively large offices and support staff, signing formal decisions and assigning authorities and resources. As a matter of fact, as previously noted, with the need to display a collective system of decision making as well as an informal form of hierarchy, many of the leaders of the alternative globalization movement were constantly required to function from the penumbra. Nevertheless, their presence was indispensable in making important decisions, putting into operation major activities and handling matters relating to critical organizational communications. The majority of these leaders originated from the Northern countries, primarily from Europe. Many of them had roots in the academic, professional and NGO world; and they were previously connected to traditional forms of political mobilization such as those mounted by political parties and trade union organizations. Several of these features were also commonly present among the leaders originating from the Southern developing countries. In any event, both groups of leaders came invariably from a middle class social background.

Undeniably, some of these elements have remained common characteristics among leaders in numerous other types of social movements in the recent past[1] (see Offe 1985: 817–868). With specific reference to the alternative globalization movement, a dimension particularly worth noting was that, since critical resources and decision-making power were concentrated at the highest level, the movement's central leaders were in a most advantageous position to acquire and control important organizational power by simply clinging onto a small international organ. This was perceptibly evident in the case of the WSF leaders and their capacity to stay on at the IC, but this situation was not significantly different with respect to the four transnational campaigns as well. Besides, the absence of clear administrative regulations and systems of political representations, a common feature of the entire alternative globalization movement was that leaders from both these movements were able to enjoy authority and power without usually requiring that they justify their conduct or performance, as well as the ensued outcomes affecting the organization as a whole.

THE EXERCISE OF POWER TAKES PLACE WHILE DENYING IT

From its inception, the alternative globalization movement in its general makeup emphasized a political vision aimed at rejecting the internal formation and exercise of power, with the organization's entire ideology and working methods being directed to achieving this very goal. It was with this conception in mind that certain anti-neoliberal ideologues suggested the prospect for bringing about major political changes without seizing any power[2] (cf. Holloway 2005). In this work, we found that there was indeed a significant practice of producing, accumulating and utilizing power within the organization, while, at the same time, the movement continued to evoke its sweeping disapproval to the very notion and internal exercise of power.

The relationship between what was intended (or might be announced) and what actually happened in reality need to be better understood. In the case of the alternative globalization movement, once the concept of power that could potentially produce formalization, hierarchy and undue influence by a few was rejected, internal power relations within the movement were considered to be *ipso facto* absent. Michels had insisted that "even in groups sincerely animated with the democratic spirit, current business, the preparation and the carrying out of the most important actions, is necessarily left in the hands of individuals (Michels 1959: 27). Likewise, in the early 1950s, Selznick emphasized that "taking on of values" and "ways of acting" were two different organizational outcomes. To him, in attempting to "preserve the uniqueness of the group in the face of new problems and altered circumstances," "self-maintenance becomes more than bare organizational survival," hence the rise of an institutionalization with the attribution of tasks, delegations of authority and power to certain individuals (Selznick 1957: 20–21). With regard to the alternative globalization movement, the illustrations and assessments presented earlier underscored that it was precisely the need to ensure that the essential activities continued to happen that a certain number of individuals began to acquire important

responsibilities and steadily increased their influence over the organization. Progressively, an important fissure began to occur between the initial
organizational canon and the incident of a growing exercise of power by a
select few, including the invention and reinforcing of a largely closed system of management.

Was there a deliberate or pre-planned attempt on the part of the key
leaders to conceive a movement from the outset so as to acquire personal
power? Was there an obsession of power exercise in a high-handed manner?
The answer is evidently no. This is also not to suggest that the movement
was completely denuded with committed individuals. Quite the opposite,
many of the leaders held a deep sense of mission and commonly looked
to strengthen the movement's expanded popularity and durability. In any
event, the fostering of a collective identity among participating individuals
and organizations and maintaining of a general steadiness in action were
as much in the personal interests of the leaders as to the broad dynamics
of the movement.

Nonetheless, a small group of individuals, frequently highly motivated
and well-informed, managed to come to the forefront and consolidated
their leadership position. In particular, with time they became increasingly
successful in their effort to access organizational resources and reinforcing
their overall decision-making capacity. Subsequently, the setting of organizational goals and activities, albeit formally suggested to be taking place on
a collective basis, turned out to be the exclusive prerogative of the leadership. At the same time, this leadership could circumvent putting in place
a transparent and openly contestable system of organizational representation. On the contrary, the movement was steadily pushed into harboring
copious ambiguities and uncertainties in order to accommodate their own
interests, as well as the emerging patterns of asymmetrical power relations
within the movement. Yet in view of upholding the general philosophical
principles, asserting an internal organizational cohesion or seeking to exert
a certain level of external influence became all the more important for these
leaders to persist affirming a formal and nearly a ritual line of interpretation
of power, including the attempt to pledge that the movement was safely
preserved from being a locus of power to the specific benefit of a small
number of individuals.

LACK OF INTERNAL RESISTANCE
TO POWER CONCENTRATION

Foucault argues that "there can be no relations of power without resistance"
(Foucault 1994: 42). Indeed, much of the Marxist analytical tradition has
deemed the "organization" to be a prime arena of managerial regulation

designed for a perpetual exploitation of labor by capital and technology, including the use of cultural influence.[3] Accordingly, divergence of class interests and conflicts were to be expected.[4] In particular, the resistance of workers was seen as an intrinsic characteristic of the modern industrial system. Observably, there was little relevance of this type of class interpretation concerning the relationship between the leadership and participant groups and individuals making the alternative globalization movement. Nevertheless, as we have clearly seen, an informal pyramidal structure was very much an organizational reality, with international coordination bodies and few individuals allowing the leadership enjoying enormous unsupervised power. At the same time, there existed no elections or the possibility of democratically challenging the leadership in place. Instead, these individuals formed a "closed community" with the ability to deciding upon all strategic matters. As a group, they therefore possessed a substantial degree of dominance to exclude people or organizations outside of this close circle from vital information, financial resources, visibility and other potential gains. At the same time, the prospects for an internal resistance to power concentration appeared seemingly low. So the question arises: Why was this actually so?

There were indeed various reasons for this. Let us regroup the principal elements into two clusters. First, since the key individuals making the leadership commanded a great deal of eminence and legitimacy, the different branches, groups or individuals associated with the movement felt, even when dissatisfied, a general psychological barrier against being unkind and ignoble towards their leaders. Already many leaders maintained a high moral authority since they would usually have made a considerable degree of personal sacrifices in terms of their time, family life and financial resources to the general benefit of the movement.[5] The leadership formed the primary custodian of organizational values; it was the source of basic discourses and expertise; it demonstrated a great deal of capacity in linking the movement to broader groups of social organizations; and it held salutary contacts with the media, supportive government elites and funding institutions. But more than anything else their legitimacy was derived from the simple fact that the very survival of the movement would not have been possible without their personal and collective engagements. Overall, the prevailing leadership stood to be nearly irreplaceable, and as such, no open internal challenge could easily crystallize against the way the authority was exercised or the movement as a whole was functioning.

Second, and perhaps even more importantly, the quintessence of international network politics implied that individual activists or their organizations could join or leave the movement when and as they desired. As a result, no significant organizational pressure could realistically be brought upon the key leaders. Instead, this situation gave the leaders a real capacity to remind opponents that the latter were obviously not obliged to stay on within the movement, if they grew unhappy with the existing organizational parameters or began to cause trouble. As a matter of fact, national level leaders were already largely neutralized though cooptation within the organizational rank and file (however informal) and through the provision of occasional financial supports. Furthermore, as the international network politics has mainly been about ensuring the symbolic presence of numerical individual participants at major global events, there was no obligation on the part of the leadership to maintain a stable membership-based representation structure as well.

In reality, the leadership itself was made in a considerably haphazard manner with the possibility of certain leaders vanishing in the multitude when necessary. In a situation where one did not know "who was in" and "who was out" in the movement, direct negotiations with the leadership could scarcely be envisaged. More fundamentally, owing to the absence of an electoral system, opponents were not in a position to utilize the power of voting to replace or partially renew the leadership. It may thus be admitted that the power and the freedom enjoyed by individuals and their organizations by virtue of voluntarily taking part in the international network politics had the downside of obstructing the emergence of a rational and robust opposition that could have ultimately helped to reduce the different forms of obscurity and the lack of internal democracy characterizing the alternative globalization movement.

Undoubtedly, the opponents held the choice of creating a parallel contending movement. Yet if they were to follow the same general model of international network politics, the final outcome could not be that different as compared to the original movement. In any event, the creation of a new social movement and in particular maintaining its durability was never an easy task. Of course, to individuals and organizations plainly dissatisfied, there was the usual alternative of simply remaining inactive within the movement. But again, little could actually be achieved or changed in the existing composition of the leadership by this way.

The dimensions of power and reciprocity have often been perceived as being mutually correlated within organizations (see, for example, Crozier and Friedberg 1977: 49–64). While a certain degree of reciprocity was also manifest between the international leadership and national organizations, the relationship was far from equal. The former maintained a marked upper hand, with national organizations being largely reduced to dependent positions. Having said this, national organizations, too, could not otherwise have hoped to acquire the prestige, visibility and external funds, however limited, which they occasionally enjoyed by virtue of being associated with the international network or organizational leadership. Naturally, unlike in the formal administration or an economic enterprise, they feared no direct reprimand from the center in the event they chose not to vigorously rally with or even criticize the leadership. This, nevertheless, implied the risk of being gradually sidelined within the network. For the most part, thus, the lower echelons tended to have a much reduced reciprocity function, particularly in its capacity to produce any significant countervailing power within the organization.

FINAL REMARKS

Organizations have frequently been viewed as being equal to power. We briefly referred earlier to the Marxist conception on this. But industrial or management specialists, too, have commonly recognized that within organizations, power remained an "obvious aspect" because "it is a characteristic of one's position in the chain of command and the official or formal rights attached to that position" (Handel 2003: 205). Combining empirical records and a critical review of the literature, this book has shown that the alternative globalization movement and transnational network politics in general was also about exercising of power by another name. It has demonstrated how numerous forms of organizational structure, legitimacy, leadership, zones of uncertainty and representation systems were created in order to help attain and uphold power by a small group of individuals at the international level.

So far as the formal organizational notion of power was concerned, the alternative globalization movement did stand out to be quite different as compared to most political and labor movements in the past, in that it openly rejected both the internal formation as well as instrumentalization of the movement for the purpose of grabbing institutional political power. All the same, power was deeply manifest inside the organization. Is not this then a simple charlatan, as Stendhal inferred (cited as an opening quote in the book): i.e., to proclaim formally that power was disconcerting but allow in practice power concentration to largely transpire? Undoubtedly, the movement's original political vision attached considerable importance to an imaginative organization structure. However, as the movement moved towards an enhanced degree of "institutionalization" with the requirement of handling different sets of basic activities, the organizational authority and resources were progressively assigned to specific individuals at the international level. This situation steadily led to the emergence of a permanent leadership with the capacity to create procedures and other astute mechanisms so as to ensure, among other things, its own continued grip on power.

Overall, it has proven markedly easier for the alternative globalization movement to criticize the existing patterns of external or wider structures of power than to deal with the internal processes of a growing incidence of power and its appropriation by a select few at the peak of the hierarchy. At the same time, a bare insistence on its primary conviction, however valiant it may be, that the movement was free of internal power relations would scarcely help to change the situation. Quite the reverse, recognizing that the movement has leaders, a certain degree of hierarchy and resources, and aided by the instauration of a more structured form of membership base and a transparent representation system could potentially help to impede the processes of any undue power concentration and oligarchic tendencies within the movement. Of course, if this happened, some of those who made up the existing leadership would surely stand to lose. Ironically, the resistance to organizational change might actually come from those who characteristically called for deep social transformation. Here lies a major complication. In addition to this, the experience of participatory democracy in the past decades has suggested that professionalism, formalization and bureaucratic logic can in fact "kill" the very "engagement and purity of intentions" (Sainsaulieu 2001: 158).

As noted in the beginning of this essay, many scholars who considered the alternative globalization movement as a singular phenomenon, owing to its imaginative political philosophy and initial mobilization capacity, have frequently ignored most of these complexities relating to the internal dimension of power. This work has attempted to make the case that organizational power was a real issue not only within formal organizations but also within informal international networks and coalition groups seeking to vehicle utopian projects. And this seemed to be largely so irrespective of what the organizations themselves announced or even insisted.

It has not been the scope of the present work to find out whether the concentration of power in the hands of a select few at the top has had an impeding consequence to the global efficacy of the movement. Nevertheless, a careful examination of the organizational life of the movement pointed strongly towards the emergence of a major contradiction in its original mission that aimed at making the movement an open, equitable space for all participating groups and organizations and its gradual alteration into an important source of power for the benefit of a small number of individuals making the leadership. This trend towards the accumulation of power was particularly worrisome given that the movement's very uniqueness relied on its ability to formulate an innovative construal of power, particularly its proposition to distribute power across various social organizations making the movement. Equally worrisome was that this trend seemed to have been intricately linked to the movement's attempt to implement its core values and a minimum number of essential activities. Was the movement's organizational life then condemned to be beset by this critical tension between the need to display fundamental values, including its innovative interpretations on power, on the one hand, and the operationalization evolutions that tended to largely subdue them, on the other? Based on the evidence and analyses presented here, the prognostic was rather palpable, hence the necessity for continuous theorizing, empirical research and detached reflections on the evolving organizational life and societal potency of the movement, as well as the transnational network politics in general.

NOTES

1. Typically these included peace movements, environmental campaigns and feminist activism.

2. It may be noted that the anarchistic conception of power to which Holloway seems to plainly adhere has consistently rejected the seizure of State power to be the ultimate political strategy for a social mobilization.

3. Gramsci argued that the maintaining of hegemony by the ruling class depended not only on their sway over economic and political power, but also their control over the "private" apparatus of "hegemony" or "civil society" (Gramsci 1976: 261). For Gramsci, the latter dimension notably included educational institutions, cultural practices, as well as associative structures.

4. For an overview of these debates, see Chanlat and Séguin 1987: 2–35.

5. Some of the leaders have no doubt also managed to personally access new resources by mobilizing around the alternative globalization movement such as the beneficial contacts with the press, international intellectual circles and funding agencies. In certain cases, they have also been able to offer their "expertise" to public authorities and enterprises claiming to be socially responsible.

Bibliography

Abers, Rebecca. "From Clientelism to Cooperation: Local Government, Participatory Policy and Civil Organizing in Porto Alegre, Brazil." *Politics and Society*, Vol. 26, No. 4, 1998.

Abinales, Patricio and Donna Amoroso. *State and Society in the Philippines.* Lanham: Rowman & Littlefield, 2005.

AER. *Documentation of Proceedings of International Workshop on Capital Flows: Arresting Speculation and Volatility.* Hong Kong: AER/Asian Regional Exchange for New Alternatives, 2001.

Afrobarometer. http://www.forumcivil.sn/spip.php?article36# (accessed on January 12, 2009).

AGP. http://www.agp.org (accessed May 12, 2010).

Agrikoliansky, Eric, Olivier Fillieule and Nonna Mayer. *L'Altermondialisme en France.* Paris: Flammarion, 2005.

Agrikoliansky, Eric and Isabelle Sommier. *Radiographie du mouvement altermondialiste.* Paris: La Dispute, 2005.

Albert, Michael. "WSF: Where to Now." http://www.countercurrents.org/wsf-albert 2403.html (accessed April 18, 2010).

Almeyra, Guillermo. *Rébellions d'Argentine.* Paris: Editions Syllepse, 2006.

Alternative libertaire. http://www.alternativelibertaire.org (accessed May 12, 2010).

Amin, Samir. "Le Forum Social Mondial est-il utile pour les luttes populaires?" http://www.forumsocialmundial.org.br/noticias_textos.php?cd_news=349 (accessed February 10, 2010).

Ancelovici, Marcos. "Organizing against Globalization: The Case of Attac in France." *Politics & Society*, Vol. 30, No. 3, September 2002.

Ariate, Joel and Ronald Molmisa. "More Than Debt Relief: Two Decades of Freedom from Debt Coalition." In *Localizing and Transnationalizing Contentious Politics: Global Civil Society Movements in the Philippines,* edited by Teresa Tadem, Lanham: Lexington Books, 2009.

Attac. *Le petit alter: Dictionnaire altermondialiste*. Paris: Mille et Une Nuits, 2006.

Attac. http://www.attac.org/spip.php?article.8206 (accessed May 12, 2010).

Attac France. http://www.france.attac.org/spip.php?articles8326 (accessed September 14, 2009).

Attac Senegal. http://www.attac.org/senegal/calandrier.html (accessed January 11, 2010).

Auyero, Javier. "Glocal Riots," *International Sociology*, Vol. 16, No. 1, March 2001.

Auyero, Javier. "Protest and Politics in Contemporary Argentina." In *Argentine Democracy*, edited by Steven Levitsky and Maria Murillo, University Park: The Pennsylvania State University Press, 2005.

Balisacan, Arsenio and Hal Hill. *The Philippine Economy*. New York: Oxford University Press, 2003.

BBC. http://www.news.bbc.com.uk/2/hi/business/4533740.stm (accessed May 5, 2010).

Bello, Walden, Herbert Docena, Marissa de Guzman and Marylou Laig. *The Anti-Developmental State: The Political Economy of Permanent Crisis in the Philippines*. Quezon City: University of the Philippines and Focus on the Global South, 2004.

Bidaseca, Karina and Federico Rossi. "Coaliciones nacionales contra procesos continentales de liberalización comercial: la Autoconvocatoria No al ALCA." In *Conflictos globales, voces locales*, edited by Alejandro Grimson and Sebastián Pereyra. Buenos Aires: Prometeo Libros, 2008.

Bloch, Maurice. *Political Language and Oratory in Traditional Society*. London: Academy Press, 1975.

Bonfond, Olivier. http://www.forumsocialmundial.org.br/noticias_textos.php?cd_news=357 (accessed January 10, 2010).

Bourdieu, Pierre. *Contre-feux 2*. Paris: Editions Raisons d'Agir, 2001.

Braudel, Fernand. *La grammaire des civilisations*. Paris: Flammarion, 1987.

Cabilo, Zuraida. "From North to South: Campaigning for Fair Trade in the Philippines." In *Localizing and Transnationalizing Contentious Politics: Global Civil Society Movements in the Philippines*, edited by Teresa Tadem, Lanham: Lexington Books, 2009.

Calvet, Louis-Jean. *Le marché aux langues: Les effets linguistiques de la mondialisation*. Paris: Plon, 2002.

Cassen, Bernard. *Tout a commencé à Porto Alegre*. Paris: Mille et Une Nuits, 2003.

Cassen, Bernard. "Repenser les forums sociaux." *Libération*. January 12, 2004.

Chabal, Patrick and Jean-Pascal Daloz. *L'Afrique est partie! Du désordre comme instrument politique*. Paris: Economica, 1999.

Chanlat, Jean-François and Francine Séguin. *L'analyse des organisations une anthologie sociologique*. Québec: Gaëtan morin, 1987.

Clegg, Stewart. *Frameworks of Power*. London: Sage, 1989.

Clegg, Stewart. "'Lives in the Balance': A Comment on Hinings and Greenwood's Disconnects and Consequences in Organization Theory?" *Administrative Science Quarterly* Vol. 47, No. 3, September 2002.

Collins, Carole, Gariyo Zie and Tony Burdon. "Jubilee 2000: Citizen Action Across the North-South Divide." In *Global Citizen Action*, edited by Michael Edwards and John Gaventa. London: Earthscan, 2001.

Corsetti, Giancarlo. "Paper Tigers? A Model of the Asian Crisis?" *European Economic Review*, 43, No. 7, June 1999.

Crozier, Michel. *Le phénomène bureaucratique*. Paris: Seuil, 1963.

Crozier, Michel and Erhard Friedberg. *L'acteur et le système*. Paris: Seuil, 1977.

Daffé, Gaye. "La difficulté réinsertion du Sénégal dans le commerce mondial." In *La société sénégalaise entre le local et le global*, edited by Momar-Cumba Diop. Paris: Karthala, 2002.

Daffé, Gaye. "La problématique des taxations pour le développement." In *Mouvements sociaux contemporains à l'échelle mondiale et locale: Le cas du Sénégal*, edited by Ibrahima Thioub and Babacar Diop. Geneva: UNRISD, 2007 (unpublished manuscript).

Dansokho, Mamadou. "L'impact de la libéralisation des filières de production." In *Mouvements sociaux contemporains à l'échelle mondiale et locale: Le cas du Sénégal*, edited by Ibrahima Thioub and Babacar Diop. Geneva: UNRISD, 2007 (unpublished manuscript).

de Dios, Emmanuel and Paul Hutchcroft. "Political Economy." In *The Philippine Economy*, edited by Arsenio Balisacan and Hal Hill. New York: Oxford University Press, 2003.

DEF. http://www.weforum.org/pdf/SummaryReports/Davos_report.pdf (accessed May 24, 2010).

della Porta, Donatella. *The Social Bases of the Global Justice Movement: Some Theoretical Reflections and Empirical Evidence from the First European Social Forum*. Geneva: UNRISD, 2005.

Dembele, Demba Moussa. *Debt and Destruction in Senegal*. London: World Development Movement, 2003; http://www.wdm.org.uk/resources/reports/debt/senegal 01112003.pdf (accessed January 11, 2010).

De Paula, Silvana. *De Rio-92 au Forum Social Mundial: O impacto de reunioes internacionais da ONU sobre na sociedade civil Brasileira*. Geneva: UNRISD, 2006 (unpublished manuscript).

Diaz, Liliana. "Resources for Creating Another World: Financial Strategies of the World Social Forum." *Development*, Vol. 29, No. 2, June 2006.

Diop, Babacar. "Le commerce équitable." In *Mouvements sociaux contemporains à l'échelle mondiale et locale : Le cas du Sénégal*, edited by Ibrahima Thioub and Babacar Diop. Geneva: UNRISD, 2007 (unpublished manuscript).

Dubet, François and Henri Thaler. "Introduction: The Sociology of Collective Action Reconsidered." *Current Sociology*, Vol. 52 (4), 2004.

El Deber. "Mapa para seguir a los medios," June 2, 2001.

Epstein, Edward and David Pion-Berlin. "The Crisis of 2001 and Argentine Democracy." In *Broken Promises: The Argentine Crisis and Argentine Democracy*, edited by Epstein Edward and David Pion-Berlin. Lanham: Lexington Books, 2006.

Focus on the Global South. http://www.focusweb.org/main/html (accessed May 12, 2010).

Foucault, Michel. *Dits et écrits* (1976-79; Volume III). Paris: Gallimard, 1994.

Foucault, Michel. "Method." In *The Global Resistance Reader*, edited by Louise Amoore. London: Routledge, 2005.

Foweraker, Joe, Todd Landman and Neil Harvey. *Governing Latin America*. Cambridge: Polity, 2003.

Franco, Patrice. *The Puzzle of Latin American Economic Development*. Lanham: Rowman & Littlefield, 2007.

Freire, Paulo. *Pedagogy of the Oppressed.* New York: Seabury, 1970.

Galtung, Fredrik. "A Global Network to Curb Corruption: The Experience of Transparency International." In *The Third Force: The Rise of Transnational Civil Society,* edited by Ann Florini. Tokyo and Washington, D.C.: Japan's Centre for International Exchange and Carnegie Endowment for International Peace, 2000.

Galvan, Dennis. "Political Turnover and Social Change in Senegal." *Journal of Democracy,* Vol. 12, No. 3, July 2001.

Gellar, Sheldon. *Democracy in Senegal.* Basingstoke: Palgrave Macmillan, 2005.

George, Susan. "The global citizens movement." *New Agenda,* Issue 6, Second quarter, 2002.

Ghimire, Kléber. "Introduction: Financial Independence among NGOs and Social Movements." *Development,* 49 (2), June 2006.

Ghimire, Kléber. "The United Nations World Summits and Civil Society Activism: Grasping the Centrality of National Dynamics." *European Journal of International Relations,* March 2010.

Ghimire, Kléber. "The Alterglobalization Movement: A New Humanism? A Case of the World Social Forum." In *Beyond Development and Globalization: Social Movement & Critical Perspectives,* edited by Dominique Caouette and Dip Kapoor. Ottawa: University of Ottawa Press, (forthcoming).

Giordano, Thierry. *Fiscalité internationale et financement du développement durable.* Paris: Institut du développement durable et des relations internationales, 2004.

Gramsci, Antonio. *Selections from the Prison Notebooks.* London: Lawrence and Wishart, 1976.

Grimson, Alejandro and Sebastián Pereyra. *Conflictos globales, voces locales.* Buenos Aires: Prometeo Libros, 2008a.

Grimson, Alejandro and Sebastián Pereyra. "Introducción: Sobre las heterogeneidades de lo transnacional y los marcos interpretativos." In *Conflictos globales, voces locales,* edited by Alejandro Grimson and Sebastián Pereyra. Buenos Aires: Prometeo Libros, 2008b.

Grzybowski, Candido. "Why Reflect on the World Social Forum?," *Democracia Viva,* January 2003.

Guidry John, Michael Kennedy and Mayer Zald. *Globalizations and Social Movements.* Ann Arbor: The University of Michigan Press, 2000.

Hadjadj, Djilali. *Combattre la corruption: Enjeux et perspectives.* Paris: Karthala, 2002.

Handel, Michael. *The Sociology of Organizations.* London: Sage, 2003.

Hardt, Michael and Antonio Negri. *Multitude: Guerre et démocratie à l'âge de l'empire.* Paris: La Découverte, 2004.

Hatch, Mary and Ann Cunliff. *Théorie des organisations.* Brussels: De Boeck, 2009.

Hedman, Eva-Lotta. *In the Nature of Civil Society.* Honolulu: University of Hawaii Press, 2006.

Hinings, C.R. and Royston Greenwood. "Disconnects and Consequences in Organization Theory?" *Administrative Science Quarterly* Vol. 47, No. 3, September 2002.

Holloway, John. *Change the World Without Taking Power.* London: Pluto Press, 2005.

Hopkins, A.G. "The History of Globalization—and the Globalization of History?" In *Globalization in World History,* edited by Hopkins, A.G. London: Pimlico, 2002.

Houtard, François. "The World Social Forum in Nairobi," http://www.forumsocial mundial.org.br/noticias_textos.php?cd_news=354 (accessed February 10, 2010).

IICG. http://www.peoplesgovernance.org (accessed May 12, 2010).

Jervolino, Domenico with Alex Callinicos et al. "Que pensent les marxistes de l'altermondialisme? *Actuel Marx* Number 44, 2nd Semester, 2008.

Kang, David. *Crony Capitalism: Corruption and Development in South Korea and the Philippines.* Cambridge: Cambridge University Press, 2002.

Kech, Margaret and Kathryn Sikkink. *Activists beyond Borders.* Ithaca: Cornell University press, 1998.

Keet, Dot. "The International Anti-Debt Campaign: A Southern Activist View for Activists in 'the North' . . . and 'the South.'" In *Debating Development, NGOs and the Future*, edited by Deborah Eade and Ernst Ligteringen. Oxford: Development in Practice Book Series. Oxfam Great Britain, 2001.

Kim, Young-Chul. "Understanding the Silence Amid Turmoil: The Tobin Tax and East Asia." In *Debating the Tobin Tax*, edited by Weaver, James, Randall Dodd and Jamie Baker. Washington, D.C.: New Rules for Global Finance Coalition, 2003.

Kohl, Benjamin and Linda Farthing. *Impasse in Bolivia.* London: Zed Books, 2006.

Kuhn, Alfred and Robert Beam. *The Logic of Organization.* San Francisco: Jossey Bass Publishers, 1982.

Kuper, Andrew. *Democracy beyond Borders.* Oxford: Oxford University Press, 2004.

Lamberte, Mario. *Currency Crisis: Where Do We Go from Here?* Makati City: Human Development Network, 1999.

Levitsky, Steven. "Argentina: Democratic Survival amidst Economic Failure." In *The Third Wave of Democratization in Latin America*, edited by Frances Hagopian and Scott Mainwaring. Cambridge: Cambridge University Press, 2005.

Martin, Dominique, Jean-Luc Metzger and Philippe Pierre. "The Sociology of Globalization: Theoretical and Methodological Reflections." *International Sociology*, Vol. 21 (4), July 2006.

Massiah, Gustave. "La réforme de l'ONU et le movement altermondialiste." *Mouvements*, 39/40, May–August, 2005.

Mayorga, Fernando and Eduardo Córdova. *El Movimiento antiglobalización en Bolivia.* La Paz: Plural Editors, 2008.

Mayorga, René. "Bolivia's Democracy at the Crossroads." In *The Third Wave of Democratization in Latin America*, edited by Frances Hagopian and Scott Mainwaring. Cambridge: Cambridge University Press, 2005.

McAdam, Dough, John McCarthy, Mayer Zald. *Comparative Perspectives on Social Movements.* Cambridge: Cambridge University Press, 1996.

McCarthy, John and Mayer Zald. *The Trend of Social Movements in America: Professionalization and Resource Mobilization.* Morristown: General Learning Press, 1973.

Medalla, Felipe. "Economic Integration in East Asia: A Philippine Perspective." In *East Asian Visions: Perspectives on Economic Development*, edited by Gill Indermit, Yukon Huang and Homi Kharas. Washington, D.C.: World Bank and Institute of Policy Studies, 2007.

Media, Juan Abal. "The Argentina Political Crisis and Necessary Institutional Reform." In *Broken Promises: The Argentine Crisis and Argentine Democracy*, edited by Edouard Epstein and David Pion-Berlin. Lanham: Lexington Books, 2006.

Melucci, Alberto. "The Symbolic Challenge of Contemporary Movements." *Social Research*, Vol. 52, No. 4, Winter 1985.

Melluci, Alberto. *Challenging Codes: Collective Action in the Information Age*. Cambridge: Cambridge University Press, 1996.

Michels, Robert. *Political Parties: A Sociological Study of the Oligarchical Tendencies of Modern Democracy*. New York: Dover Publications, 1959.

Mintzberg, Henry. *Le pouvoir dans les organisations*. Paris: Editions d'Organisation, 2003.

Molmisa, Ronald. "A Movement Whose Time has not Come: Philippine Social Movements and the Tobin Tax Agenda." In *Localizing and Transnationalizing Contentious Politics: Global Civil Society Movements in the Philippines*, edited by Teresa Tadem. Lanham: Lexington Books, 2009.

Morena, Edouard. *Campaign or "Movement of Movements"? Attac France and the Currency Transaction Tax*. Geneva: UNRISD, 2007, Geneva (unpublished document).

Nardacchione, Gabriel. *Contester en infériorité en Argentine*. Paris: L'Harmattan, 2006.

National Institute of Statistics (Bolivia): http://www.udape.gov.bo/notas%20de%20coyuntura/Notas3.pdf (accessed February 14, 2010).

Nieto, Francisco. "Desmitificando la corrupcion en América Latina." *Nueva Sociedad*, November–December, 2004.

Nye, James. "Corruption and Political Development: A Cost-Benefit Analysis." *American Political Science Review*, Vol. 61, No. 2, 1967.

OECD. The Multilateral Agreement on Investment. Paris: OECD, 1998, http://www1.oecd.org/daf/mai/pdf/ng/ng987r1e.pdf.

Offe, Claus. "New Social Movements: Challenging the Boundaries of Institutional Politics." *Social Research*, Vol. 52, No. 4, Winter, 1985.

Olson, Mancur. *The Logic of Collective Action*. Cambridge: Harvard University Press, 1965.

Oxfam Great Britain. *Rigged Rules and Double Standards: Trade, Globalisation, and the Fight against Poverty* (Summary). Oxford: Oxfam Great Britain, 2002.

Patomäki, Hekki. *Global Tax Initiatives: The Movement for the Currency Transaction Tax*. Geneva: UNRISD, 2007.

Paul, James and Katarina Wahlberg. *Global Taxes for Global Priorities*. Berlin: World Economy, Ecology & Development Association/Heinrich Böll Foundation, 2002.

Peeler, John. *Building Democracy in Latin America*. Boulder: Lynne Rienner, 2004.

Pereyra, Sebastián. "La lucha contra la corrupción y las políticas de transparencia: Un programa global, un problema local." In *Conflictos globales, voces locales*, edited by in Alejandro Grimson and Sebastián Pereyra. Bueonos Aires: Prometeo Libros, 2008.

Peruzzotti, Enrique. "Demanding Accountable Government: Citizens, Politicians, and the Perils of Representative Democracy in Agentina." In *Argentine Democracy*, edited by Steven Levitsky and Maria Murillo. University Park: The Pennsylvania State University Press, 2005.

Pfeffer, Jeffrey. *Power in Organizations*. Boston: Pitman, 1981.

Plato. *La république*. Paris: Garnier Flammarion, 1966.

Quinsaat, Sharon. "Glocal Issues, Local Target: The Campaign against a New WTO Round in the Philippines." In *Localizing and Transnationalizing Contentious Politics: Global Civil Society Movements in the Philippines*, edited by Teresa Tadem. Lanham: Lexington Books, 2009.

Ramonet, Ignacio. "Günter Holzman est mort." *Le monde diplomatique*, February 2001.

Rapoport, Mario. "Entre le Mercosur et l'ALCA: L'Argentine et le protectionnisme des Etats-unis." *Alternative sud*, Vol. X, No. 1, 2003.

Rivkin, Ana. "Las mil caras de la movilización social contra el pago de la deuda externa en la Argentina." In *Conflictos globales, voces locales*, edited by Alejandro Grimson and Sebastián Pereyra. Buenos Aires: Prometeo Libros, 2008.

Robinson, Mark. "Corruption and Development: An Introduction." *European Journal of Development Research*, Vol. 10, No. 1, June 1998.

Rossi, Federico. "La transnacionalización Norte-Sur de los conflictos y sus actores: La experiencia de la red ATTAC en la Argentina." In *Conflictos globales, voces locales*, edited by Alejandro Grimson and Sebastián Pereyr. Buenos Aires: Prometeo Libros, 2008.

Rousseau, Jean-Jacques (1781) http://classiques.uqac.ca/classiques/Rousseau_jj/essai_origine_des_langues/origine_des_langues.pdf (accessed February 10, 2010).

Russell, Bertrand. *Power: A New Social Analysis*. London: Unwin Paperbacks, 1985.

Sainsaulieu, Renaud. *Des sociétés en mouvement*. Paris : Desclée De Brouwer, 2001.

Sehm-Patomäki, Katarira and Marko Ulvila. *Democratic Politics Globally*. Tampere: Network Institute for Global Democratization, 2006.

Seligson, Mitchell. "The Measurement and Impact of Corruption Victimization: Survey Evidence from Latin America." *World Development*, Vol. 34, No. 2, 2006.

Selznick, Philip. *Leadership on Administration*. Illinois/New York: Row, Peterson and Company, 1957.

Sen, Jai. "A Long March to Another World." In *Challenging Empires*, edited by Jai Sen, Anita Anand, Arturo Escobar and Peter Waterman. New Delhi: The Viveka Foundation, 2004.

Senegalese Social Forum. http://www.forumcivil.sn/spip.php?article1 (accessed September 14, 2009).

Sidibé, Doudou. *Démocratie et alternance politique au Sénégal*. Paris: L'Harmattan, 2006.

Smith, Jackie. *Social Movement for Global Democracy*. Baltimore: John Hopkins University Press, 2007.

Stendhal. *De l'amour*. Paris: Garnier, 1959.

Suarez, Hugo José. "Bolivie: Les antécédents et les défies de la nouvelle gauche." *Alternatives sud*, Vol. 12, No. 2, 2005.

Svampa, Maristella. "Argentine: l'avenir des piqueteros." *Alternative sud*, Vol. 12, No. 2, 2005.

Tadem, Teresa. (eds.). *Localizing and Transnationalizing Contentious Politics: Global Civil Society Movements in the Philippines*. Lanham: Lexington Books, 2009a.

Tadem, Teresa. "Introduction: Examining Global Civil Society Movements in the Philippines." In *Localizing and Transnationalizing Contentious Politics: Global Civil Society Movements in the Philippines*, edited by Teresa Tadem. Lanham: Lexington Books, 2009b.

Tadem, Teresa. "Localizing and Globalizing Advocacies and Alternatives: A Comparative Analysis of Five Global Civil Society Movements (A Synthesis)." In *Localizing and Transnationalizing Contentious Politics: Global Civil Society Movements in the Philippines*, edited by Teresa Tadem. Lanham: Lexington Books, 2009c.

Tagle, Yovana amd Katarina Sehm-Patomäki. *The Rise and Development of the Global Debt Movements*. Geneva: UNRISD, 2007.

Tarrow, Sydney. *The New Transnational Activism*. New York: Cambridge University Press, 2005.

Tarrow, Sydney and Doug McAdam. "Scale Shift in Transnational Contention." In *Transnational Protest and Global Activism*, edited by Donatella della Porta and Sydney Tarrow. Lanham: Rowman and Littlefield, 2005.

Tedesco, Laura. *Democracy in Argentina*. London: Frank Cass, 1999.

Teivainen, Teivo. "Democratizing the World: Reflections after Porto Alegre." In *Political Initiatives to Democratic Globalization*, edited by Rikkilä Leena and Katarina Sehm-Patomäki. Nottingham and Tampere: Network Institute for Global Democratization and Nottingham Trent University, 2001.

Teivainen, Teivo. "The World Social Forum and Global Democratization: Learning from Porto Alegre." *Third World Quarterly*, Vol. 23, No 4, 2002.

Teivainen, Teivo. "The World Social Forum: Arena or Actor?" In *Challenging Empires*, edited by Jai Sen, Anita Anand, Arturo Escobar and Peter Waterman. New Delhi: The Viveka Foundation, 2004.

The Ecologist. "Is Oxfam Right to Insist That Increased Access to Northern Markets Is a Solution to the Third World's Problems?," Vol. 32, No. 6, July–August, 2002.

Thioub, Ibrahima. "La lutte contre la corruption." In *Mouvements sociaux contemporains à l'échelle mondiale et locale : Le cas du Sénégal*, edited by Ibrahima Thioub and Babacar Diop. Geneva: UNRISD, 2007 (unpublished manuscript).

Thioub, Ibrahima and Babacar Diop. *Mouvements sociaux contemporains à l'échelle mondiale et locale : Le cas du Sénégal*. Geneva: UNRISD, 2007 (unpublished manuscript).

Third World Resurgence. No. 157/158, September-October, 2003.

Touraine, Alain. *La voix et le regard: Sociologie des mouvements sociaux*. Paris: Seuil, 1978.

Touraine, Alain. "An Introduction to the Study of Social Movements." *Social Research*, Vol. 52, No. 4, Winter 1985.

Touraine, Alain. *Un nouveau paradigme*. Paris: Fayard, 2005.

Transparency International. *Global Corruption Report 2007*. Cambridge: Cambridge University Press, 2007.

Transparency International. http://www.transparency.org.policy_research/surveys_indices/ (accessed May 5, 2010).

Uemura, Takehiko. "Exploring Potential of Global Tax: As a Cutting Edge-Measure for Democratizing Global Governance." *International Journal of Public Affairs*, Vol. 3, 2007.

UNCTAD. *Economic Development in Africa: Rethinking the Role of Foreign Direct Investment*. New York and Geneva: United Nations, 2005.

Wallerstein, Immanuel. *European Universalim*. New York and London: The New Press, 2006.

Wang, Hongying and James Rosenau. "Transparency International and Corruption as an Issue of Global Governance." *Global Governance*, Vol. 7, Issue 1, January-March 2001.

Whitaker, Chico. *Changer le monde*. Paris: Les éditions de l'atelier, 2006.

Wieviorka, Michel. *Un autre monde . . . Contestations, dérives et surprises dans l'antimondialisation*. Paris: Editions Balland, 2003.

Wolf, Martin. "Misplaced Hopes in Tobin's Tax." *Financial Times*, 20 March, 2002.

World Bank. http://www.data.worldbank.org/indicator/DT.DOD.DECT.CD (accessed May 5, 2010).

World Bank. http://www.data.worldbank.org/indicator/NE.EXP.GNFS.ZS (accessed May 5, 2010).

World Bank. http://www.data.worldbank.org/indicator/SI.DST.FRST.20 (accessed May 5, 2010).

World Bank. http://www.data.worldbank.org/indicator/NY/GDP.MKTP.KD.ZG (accessed May 5, 2010).

World Bank. http://fr.allafrica.com/stories/200802060859.html (accessed May 5, 2010).

WSF. http://www.forumsocialmundial.org.br/main.php?id_menu=3_2_2&cd_language=2 (accessed February 10, 2010).

WSF. http://www.forumsocialmundial.org.br (accessed March 15, 2010).

WSF. http://www.forumsocialmundial.org.br/main.php?id_menu=14&cd_language=2 (accessed January 10, 2010).

WSF. http://www.forumsocialmundial.org.br/noticias_01.php?cd_news=2556&cd_language=2 (accessed January 10, 2010).

WSF. http://www.forumsocialmundial.org.br/main.php?id_menu=4&cd_language=2 (accessed January 10, 2010).

WSF. http://www.forumsocialmundial.org.br/main.php?id_menu=4_2_2_1&cd_languages=2 (accessed January 10, 2010).

WSF. http://www.forumsocialmundial.org.br/dinamic.php?pagina=ci_regras_miami_ing (accessed January 10, 2010).

WSF. http://www.forumsocialmundial.org.br/download/2009-02-belem_IC_meeting_report_EN_FINAL_DRAFT.pdf (accessed January 10, 2010).

WSF. http://www.forumsocialmundial.org.br/download/carta_doacoes_FSM_por.pdf (accessed February 10, 2010).

WSF. http://www.wsflibrary.org/index.php/image:wsf-financialstrategyreport.pdf (accessed February 10, 2010).

WSF. "World Social Forum Financial Strategy." http://www.wsflibrary.org/index.php/image:wsf-financialstrategyreport.pdf (accessed February 10, 2010).

WSF. "World Social Forum Memorial." http://www.forumsocialmundial.org.br/main.php?id_menu=14_3&cd_language=2 (accessed January 10, 2010).

WSF India. "Report of the Meeting of the International Council, Miami, USA: June 23-26, 2003" (unpublished).

Wui, Ma. Glenda. "Campaigning against Corruption: The Case of the Transparency and Accountability Network." In *Localizing and Transnationalizing Contentious Politics: Global Civil Society Movements in the Philippines,* edited by Teresa Tadem. Lanham: Lexington Books, 2009.

Wui, Ma. Glenda and Teresa Tadem. *People, Profit and Politics.* Quezon City: Third World Studies Center, University of the Philippines, 2006.

Xenophon. *Œuvres completes.* Paris: Garnier Flammarion, 1967.

Index

Abers, Rebecca, 100
Abinales, Patricio, 39
academics, engaged with alternative
    globalization movement, 9, 13,
    39, 55, 56, 71; and activists on the
    left, 85; 86, Anglophone academics
    joining WSF, 88; 89, 122
Action for Economic Reforms (AER),
    57
actors: institutional, 46, 55; social, 5,
    12, 29, 57, 78, 97, 120
Administrative Science Quarterly, 6
African Network for Integrated
    Development (RADI), 51
Afrobarometer, 61, 64
Agrikoliansky, Eric, 18, 131
Albert, Michael, 131
Almeyra, Guillermo, 44
alternative globalization movement,
    initially known as anti-globalization
    movement, 3; compared with
    DEF, 10–11; general characteristics
    of, 11–14; nature and aim of, 9;
    organizational structure, 12; as a
    social organization, 3; transnational
    campaigns and WSF as two essential
    categories behind, 16–17, 18,
    20–21, 24, 62, 86–87, 89, 90, 112,

129, 131, 133–136, 138, 139–141;
    as a value-oriented organization,
    6, 7, 8. *See also* social movements;
    transnational campaigns; World
    Social Forum
alternative libertaire, 25. *See also*
    anarchist
ambiguity: in Argentinean government
    policy, 31; in content and
    course of action of transnational
    campaigns and WSF, 131; in WSF's
    organizational and decisional
    structure, 98; 126
Amin, Samir, 109, 116, 122
Amnesty International, 15
Amoroso, Donna, 39
anarchist, 13. *See also* alternative
    libertaire
Ancelovici, Marcos, 23
Andean Free Trade Agreement (AFTA),
    50, 51, 63, 71
Anglophone, transnational campaigns
    emanating from Anglophone
    developed countries, 68; Anglophone
    academics and international
    development NGOs, 88
anti-corruption campaign, 17; in
    Argentina, 57–59, 76–77; in Bolivia,

153

Lightning Source UK Ltd.
Milton Keynes UK
05 April 2011

170384UK00001B/48/P